# The Science Of Putting

How science can help you to improve your putting accuracy.

Geoff Kirby

Copyright © 2014 Geoff Kirby

All rights reserved.

ISBN-13: 978-1499357455

ISBN-10: 1499357451

# CONTENTS

|   |   |   |
|---|---|---|
|   | **Acknowledgments** | Pg v |
| 1 | **Introduction.** The philosophy behind this project - improving everyone's putting performance by the application of science. | Pg 1 |
| 2 | **The Mathematics of Putting.** The derivation of the equations of motion of a golf ball on a putting green and the experimental evidence that the deceleration of a golf ball on grass is independent of speed. | Pg 5 |
| 3 | **The Mathematical Model.** The mathematical model is derived and validated experimentally by measurements on golf courses. | Pg 25 |
| 4 | **The 'Stimpmeter'.** The 'Stimpmeter' is used professionally to measure the 'speed' of greens. Its operation is described and some of its shortcomings and limitations are explained. | Pg 35 |
| 5 | **Holing The Ball.** The math of getting the ball into the cup as a function of ball speed, dynamic characteristics of the grass rim and accuracy of aim is described. The equations are verified using an artificial cup and rolling golf balls. | Pg 41 |
| 6 | **Randomness, Skill And Mathematical Modelling.** Proof that 'holes in one' are flukes and nothing special. Sorry to disillusion Hole-in-Oners! | Pg 53 |
| 7 | **Examples Of What The Model Can Do.** Results from running a mathematical model are presented which show that the optimum technique for aiming a ball on a green is to try to stop the ball about 200 - 250 mm (6 - 8 inches) beyond the cup. More complicated techniques can be offered but this simple rule-of-thumb will suit the great majority of golfers. | Pg 61 |

# FORWARD

8 **What It All Means For The Non-Technical Player**. A summary of all the technical stuff for the non-technical reader who wants to benefit from this scientific work without the equations. Simple charts and 'rules of thumb' are presented which any golfer can use. Pg 71

9 **Appendix A - Conversion Between Metric and Imperial Units** Pg 81

10 **Appendix B - The Mathematics Of Bouncing Golf Balls** Pg 83

**References** Pg 89

References to source material are shown in square brackets [ ].

# FORWARD

*"A curious anomaly is found in a review of golf literature of the past fifty years. Ninety percent of the literature deals with moving the ball from tee to green. Although there are hundreds of books and articles published on putting they deal almost exclusively with grip, technique, and stroking the ball. Practically nothing is written on how to read the green and estimate or calculate how much a ball will break."*

— H. A. Templeton, 'Vector Putting'

To illustrate the general lack of advice in golfing books on reading greens consider the weighty *"The Complete Book Of Golf"* published by Colour Library Books. In its 520 pages the advice on putting makes up just twelve pages and most of that small section is devoted to stance and wrist action rather than reading the green. And yet it is on the putting green that shots are lost and games sacrificed.

There are eighteen tee shots in a game but a medium to high handicap player will take as many as thirty-five to fifty or more putts during a game.

Reading the green is an essential component of a successful game of golf.

This book rectifies this deficiency by explaining the way that a golf ball rolls and curves - hopefully towards the cup - after being hit. What happens after the ball is struck is outside the control of the golfer. All she can do is watch and hope she hit it to set it off at the correct speed and in the correct direction.

The math involved is no more than High School level and most golfers will be able to understand the outcome of the math modelling even if some of the equations appear a little daunting.

The equations can give insights which years of practice may not reveal. For example, the rate at which a ball veers off a straight line is inversely proportional to its speed as well as proportional to the slope. Thus, halving the ball speed doubles the rate at which the ball curves away.

In similar vein the math shows that, after a short distance during which the ball skids over the green, the rate at which a ball loses speed is constant with time. A consequence of this observation is that a ball hit twice as hard will go four times as far on a simple flat putting green.

These, and many similar simple rules, may be learned instinctively by years of dedicated practice but the equations in this book explain the math behind the experience of holing a golf ball.

# ACKNOWLEDGMENTS

This book is dedicated to Sandy - my partner in golf and life. She has tried to be enthusiastic when I stopped games of golf to measure drag coefficients with ramps a spirit level and when I filled the house with rolling golf balls at all hours of the day and night.

Thanks to Steve, who kindly tested my math model and its recommendations.

Steve has written to me as follows

*"I recently went on a 6 day golf holiday to Dubai. Every day I used a chart showing break of putt for each combination of distance to slope percentage, calculated using an amended version of your model ... to calculate the perfect putt for a given green speed, distance and slope.*

*I would say that each day I holed between 2-5 putts that I would not have holed using the naked eye to judge. That is a huge return for someone with my handicap (six) representing a saving of nearly half of my handicap each round!!"*

Praise much appreciated!

Thanks to PGA Professional Mike who patiently tried to teach me not to look like a puppet with tangled strings when on the golf course. Sorry Mike - it was not to be.

Last but not least thanks to Ryan whose mockery of my ramps and jokes about my artificial golf hole only served to spur me on to prove to him I am not completely mad.

# 1. INTRODUCTION

Early in 2010 I started to learn to play golf having never tried the game before. I had considered golf as a somewhat trivial pastime; after all, it is only about hitting a ball with a stick!

One year and two sets of lessons with a PGA level teacher later and I began to see that it may not be quite as easy as I had thought! My second ever game on an 18 hole course returned a score of 183 (114 over par) having taken 16 hits to complete some of the holes.

At the time of writing Amazon lists over 70,000 book titles relating to 'Golf' and, of these, 260 relating to 'Golf Science'

There is no substitute for practicing on a real golf course, driving range or even on the living room carpet. Golf, perhaps more than any other sport, cannot be learned from a book.

It is a rule of thumb that world quality performance in any skill takes about 10,000 hours of practice [1]. Malcolm Gladwell asserts that Bill Gates, The Beatles, Mozart, Tiger Woods and many other world leading people 'practiced' their talents for at least 10,000 hours to achieve world leadership. World leading performance comes more from long-term persistent practice and not so much on innate talent

Starting at the age of 70 and practicing golf for one hour a week (which is about what I have averaged since I first started playing) would take me over 1,300 years to achieve world leadership in the game. Put another way, playing 40 hours a week would take me over 33 years and I would be a PGA level golfer aged 103!

# INTRODUCTION

However, an understanding of the science of golf can help to improve shots. Without training, practice and insight bad habits become entrenched putting a limit on further improvement of performance.

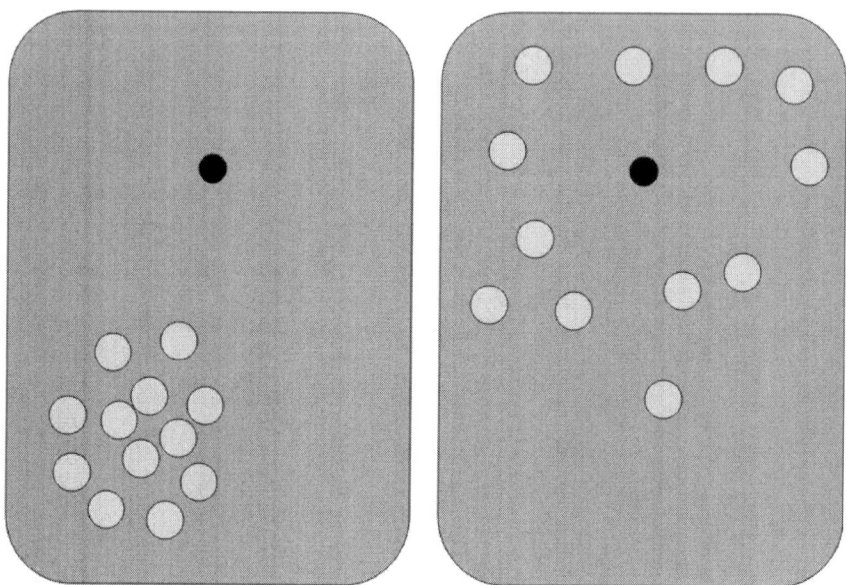

*Figure 1 - Consistency compared with Accuracy*

Let us get something straight before we start on the math and physics.

Imagine we hit a golf ball twelve times towards a target spot shown in black on the above diagrams. The end positions of the ball are marked.

On the left-hand side we have a golfer whose putting ability is good on consistency. The balls stop close to each other but the player lacks accuracy because the balls end up clustered away from the target spot. None would have ended up in the cup.

On the right-hand side of the above diagram the golfer is good on accuracy but not on consistency. The balls cluster around the target black spot. However, the spread of the points is large so few would have ended up in the cup.

A talented golfer is good on consistency and accuracy.

Consistency comes only with a great deal of practice and lessons teaching how to hold a golf club and to use it to hit the ball. Maths

# INTRODUCTION

and physics have little to offer here.

Accuracy comes from understanding how hard to hit the ball and in which direction to send it. That is what this book is about - using a knowledge of math and physics to indicate where to send the ball.

The skill in accurate putting is in 'reading' the path along which the ball must travel to reach the hole and sending the ball along that path at the correct speed.

In this study I ignore all the problems of actually hitting the ball correctly. This has been studied in great detail elsewhere. The stance, the club, the speed of the swing compared with the 'pendulum' swing speed; all have been analysed in numerous books and videos.

All I consider here is what happens after the ball sets off in a specified direction and at a specified speed.

All the golfer can do at this stage is watch and hope.

Even on nominally smooth greens there are perils that will deviate a ball from the perfect mathematical path such as rabbit droppings, leaves, worm casts, sudden wind gusts - even discarded cigarette ends blown on the wind.

However, many greens are smooth and sloping. They are inclined planes and, in principle, it is possible to compute the path of a golf ball not allowing for random irregularities and small undulations.

Having carefully inspected many golf greens it seems that, even for greens with complex changes of slope, the path from ball to hole is often over a part of the green that is fairly close to a simple inclined plane.

Although the majority of greens have a change of slope, the area having a constant slope is usually large enough such that putting to sink a ball will not result in a ball passing from a zone with one slope into an adjacent zone with a different slope.

# INTRODUCTION

*Figure 2 - A green with a single change of slope where indicated*

In any case, if the slope does change between the ball's location and the hole the mathematical model described later can include such changes.

Initially however the green will be assumed to be a simple inclined plane with no change of slope - and no rabbit droppings - to complicate the putt.

## 2. THE MATHEMATICS OF PUTTING

### 2.1 INTRODUCTION

In principle, the mathematical model described below can be used on any golf green no matter how it undulates but here it is demonstrated on a smooth inclined plane.

After a ball is hit with a putter it sets off in a certain direction and speed. From that point onwards the path of the ball is, at least in principle, predictable using mathematical equations and an EXCEL™ spreadsheet.

This model does not give advice on how to hit a ball to send it off at a given speed and direction. That is quite a different problem. This model applies only after the ball has been hit and is on its way across the green.

The model described below allows that path to be computed and indicates whether the ball will be holed or not.

For a short distance after being struck the ball skids and starts to rotate. Eventually, after a distance of about half a metre, the rotation of the ball matches the speed across the green and the ball no longer skids.

This skidding phase will be described in section 2.5.

# THE MATHEMATICS OF PUTTING

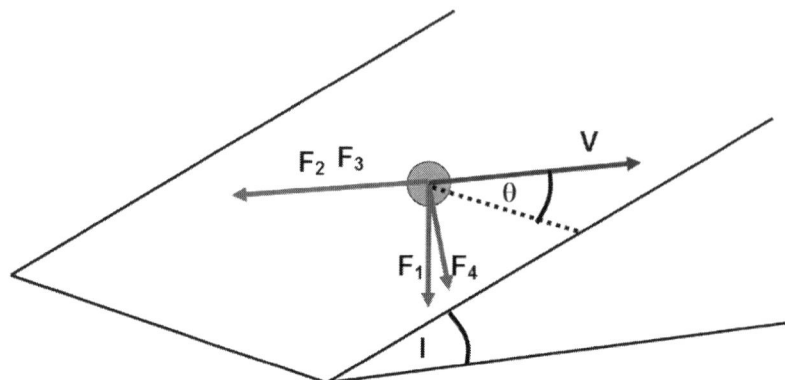

*Figure 3 - Geometry of part of an idealised putting green*

The diagram above shows the geometry of a moving golf ball on an inclined plane. The ball is moving in the direction shown by the arrow marked with speed **V** and azimuth angle $\theta$ to the horizontal direction in the plane of the surface.

There are four main forces acting on a rolling golf ball which are included in this mathematical model;

1. **Gravitational Force ($F_1$)** on the ball which acts vertically through the Centre of Gravity (**CG**) of the ball.

2. **Friction Drag ($F_2$)** due to the rolling contact of the ball with the grass. This acts in the opposite direction to the ball's motion.

3. **Air Resistance ($F_3$)** in still air due to the motion of the ball through the air adjacent to the grass. This acts in the same direction as $F_2$.

4. **Coriolis Effect ($F_4$)** causes a curving of the ball's path due to the rotation of the Earth. In effect, the green is turning in space whilst the ball moves across it and this acts like a virtual force at right angles to the ball's path acting in the horizontal plane.

There is also a fifth **Wind force.** If the wind is blowing across the green the ball will be nudged off the path it would follow in still air.

Each of the above forces except the last will be considered in turn.

## 2.2 Gravitational Force ($F_1$)

$F_1$ is the force of gravity acting vertically through the Centre of Gravity (**CG**) and has a value of **Mg** (newtons) where **M** is the mass of the ball and **g** is the acceleration due to gravity (9.81 m/s²,

32 ft/s²).

When the ball is rolling on a plane inclined at angle **I** (radians) [2] the gravitational force vector passes through a point **R**sin(**I**) down the slope from the point of contact between the ball and the inclined plane where **R** is the radius of the golf ball.

This creates a torque given by **MgR**sin(**I**) about the centre of the ball.

A rolling golf ball behaves like a gyroscope or a child's spinning top.

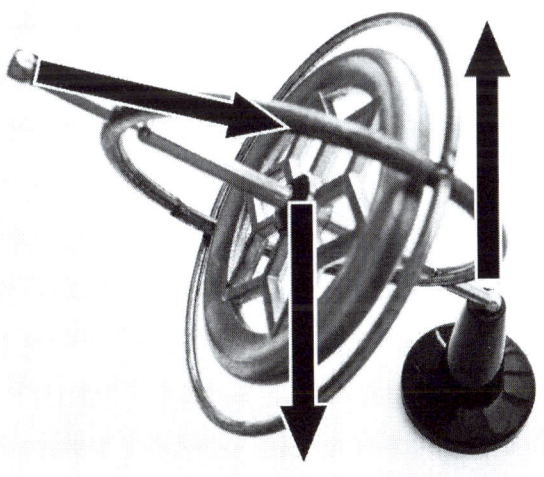

*Figure 4 - A precessing gyroscope*

Figure 4 shows a spinning gyroscope. The vertical 'down' arrow shows the force of gravity acting downwards through the Centre of Gravity (**CG**) and the 'up' arrow shows the reaction on the base acting upwards.

These two forces combine to create a torque which causes the gyroscope to precess in the horizontal plane around the fixed base as shown by the third arrow.

Now imagine the gyroscope is a golf ball rolling on an inclined plane. There is a force downwards due to gravity which acts through the **CG** but not through the point of contact with the inclined plane.

# THE MATHEMATICS OF PUTTING

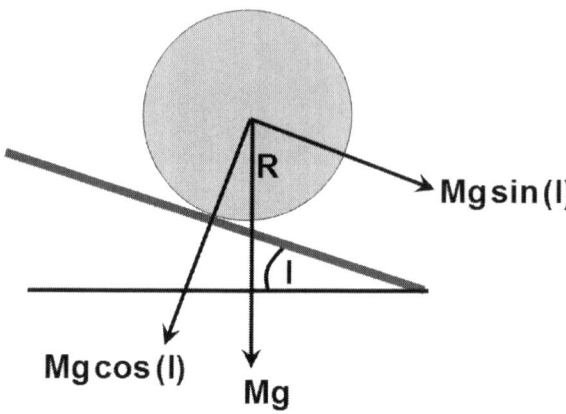

*Figure 5 - Torque on a rolling golf ball on an inclined plane*

If the ball is rolling across an inclined plane the pull of gravity causes the ball to precess and turn in a down slope direction.

For a golf ball rolling at angle θ as defined in Figure 3 the torque causing the ball to precess is

$$\Gamma = MgR \sin(I) \cos(\theta) \quad \text{(Equation 1)}$$

The following analysis of the path of a rolling golf ball is based on a study of precessional motion in a lawn bowling ball [3]. Indeed, the analysis of the trajectory of a lawn bowling ball can be easily modified to make it apply to a golf ball on an inclined plane

Lawn bowling balls have a bias generated by making the ball non-spherical as shown in Figure 6 below.

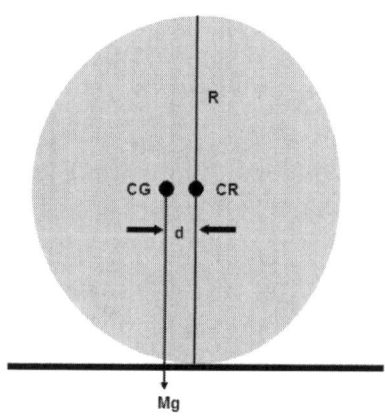

*Figure 6 - Geometry of a lawn bowling ball*

In Figure 6 **CR** is the centre of rotation and the point of contact with the horizontal lawn is directly below **CR**.

The torque is given by

$$\Gamma = Mgd \quad \text{(Equation 2)}$$

Note that the dynamics of a lawn bowling ball is equivalent to a rolling golf ball if we substitute

$$d = R\sin(I)\cos(\theta) \quad \text{(Equation 3)}$$

The torque causes the path of the lawn bowling ball to turn in the horizontal plane by a rate given by equation (3) of Cross's paper [4].

$$\frac{d\theta}{dt} = \frac{MgdR}{I_0 V} \quad \text{(Equation 4)}$$

where $I_0$ is the sum of two Moments of Inertia. The first is the Moment of Inertia about the axis of the ball's rotation and the second is the Moment of Inertia about the point of contact with the surface.

Thus

$$I_0 = \beta MR^2 + MR^2 \quad \text{(Equation 5)}$$

where $\beta = 2/5$ [5]

Substituting $R\sin(I)\cos(\theta)$ for **d** and using the above expression for $I_0$ we get

$$\frac{d\theta}{dt} = \frac{g\sin(I)\cos(\theta)}{V(1+\beta)} \quad \text{(Equation 6)}$$

where **V** is the speed of the ball.

The speed can be expressed using the conservation of energy principle. The change in potential energy due to the ball's height changing as it moves over the inclined plane is balanced by the change in total kinematic energy (translational plus rotational).

Thus

$$\frac{dV}{ds} = -\frac{g\sin(I)\sin(\theta)}{V(1+\beta)} - \frac{a}{V} \quad \text{(Equation 7)}$$

where **a** is the deceleration of the ball due to friction with the surface of the inclined plane and d**s** is the increment of distance travelled by the ball measured along the ball's path.

We will now pause because we need to know how the deceleration 'a' varies with ball speed and type of surface.

## 2.3 Drag Force in Still Air ($F_2$ and $F_3$)

The forces acting opposite to the direction the ball is moving are the drag on the ball due to the surface upon which it is rolling, **$F_2$**, and the air resistance, **$F_3$**. It is assume here that these act in the same direction and are inseparable. Hereafter, the 'drag' is assumed to be the sum of the resistance of the surface to the motion of the ball plus the air resistance in calm wind conditions.

We need to know how the drag force varies with ball speed.

The drag is a function of many variables including the condition of the grass on the green.

The effect of the force is to slow the ball down with a deceleration (negative acceleration) denoted here by **a** (m/s²) where this is a function of ball speed [6].

So, how does the drag force vary with ball speed?

This was initially tested by rolling a golf ball down an inclined wooden ramp and measuring how far it rolled along my living room carpet as a function of the speed at the end of the ramp [7].

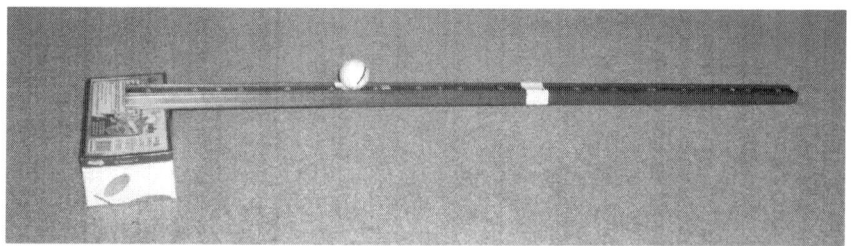

*Figure 7 - Experimental set up on my living room carpet.*

The photograph shows the set up for the measurements.

# THE MATHEMATICS OF PUTTING

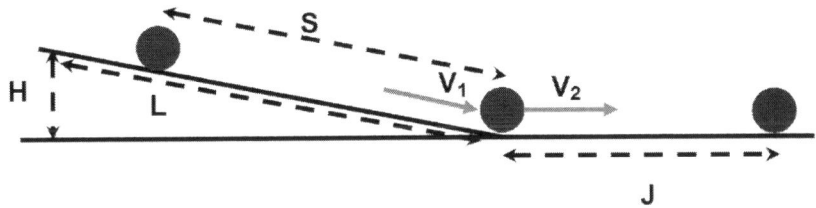

*Figure 8 - The parameters of the experiment.*

In the above diagram the variables are:-

**H** The height of the upper end of the ramp
**L** The length of the ramp
**S** The distance rolled by the ball down the ramp
**J** The distance rolled by the ball from the end of the ramp
$V_1$ The speed of the ball at the end of the ramp.
$V_2$ The speed of the ball as it starts to roll horizontally

The inclination angle of the wooden ramp was varied as well as the position of the ball on the ramp when released. The ball rolled down the ramp under the pull of gravity and the distance it rolled on the carpet was recorded.

The speed at the end of the ramp is given by

$$V_1 = \sqrt{\frac{2gH(S/L)}{1+\beta}} \quad \text{(Equation 8)}$$

where **g** is the acceleration due to gravity (9.81 m/s², 32 ft/s²) and $\beta$ is a factor depending on how much spin the ball takes up as it travels down the ramp. If the ball slides without spinning $\beta$ is zero whereas if the ball takes up its full spin whilst descending $\beta$ has the value 0.4 which is due to the moment of inertia of the ball.

A value of 0.4 was taken here for $\beta$ because the ball rolled down the slope without visible sliding.

Some of the speed at the end of the ramp is lost as the ball is deflected from the angle of the ramp into rolling motion along the ground. The correction is equal to the cosine of the angle of the ramp.

## THE MATHEMATICS OF PUTTING

Thus, the speed at which the ball sets off along the green or carpet is given by

$$V = \sqrt{\frac{2gH(S/L)}{1+\beta}\left(1-\frac{H^2}{L^2}\right)} \quad \text{(Equation 9)}$$

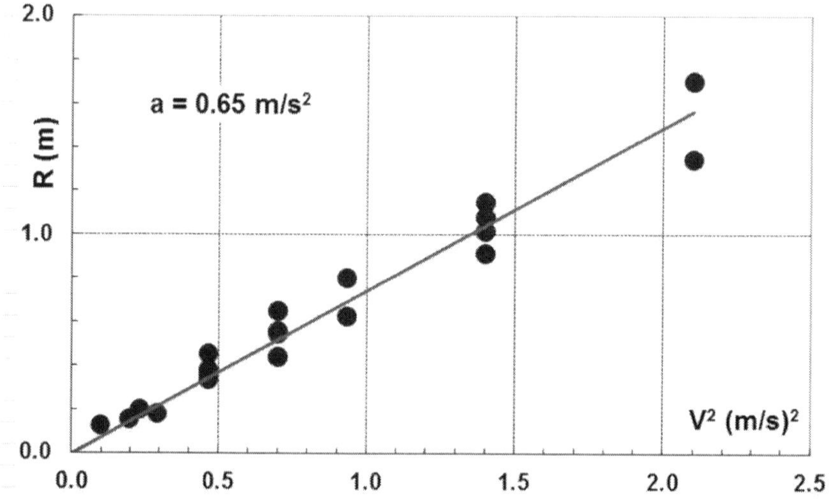

*Figure 9 - Distance rolled by golf ball along my living room carpet.*

The straight line relationship between distance travelled and square of initial speed means that the deceleration of the ball is constant and is denoted by **a** m/s². [8]

The full line on the above chart is the equation for a ball moving under constant deceleration and is given by

$$J = \frac{V^2}{2a} \quad \text{(Equation 10)}$$

where **a** is derived from the slope of the line as equal to 0.65 m/s². This is about fifteen times weaker than the downward gravitational force **g** on the golf ball.

It can be seen that the assumption of constant drag force independent of ball speed gives an excellent fit [9].

Incidentally, the energy lost by the rolling ball per unit distance rolled is given by **Ma** where **M** is the mass of the golf ball. Thus the energy needed to roll a ball over the carpet is proportional to

# THE MATHEMATICS OF PUTTING

the distance rolled. The loss of energy is probably incurred by the ball bending the carpet tufts which would give the relationship shown above.

Before going on to describe the path of a rolling ball on an inclined green we need to confirm that the same drag rule applies to a grass surface. I therefore measured the inclination 'I' and drag 'a' for a selection of golf course greens.

I took onto a local nine-hole golf course a spirit level, three blocks of wood, the ramp shown in Figure 7 above and a tape measure.

I measured the inclination of one uniformly sloping green 'I' directly with a spirit level. This came to 2.1 degrees (3.7%)

The computed horizontal speed of the ball at the end of the ramp is given by

$$V_2 = \sqrt{\frac{2gH(S/L)}{1+\beta}\left(1-\frac{H^2}{L^2}\right)} \quad \text{(Equation 11)}$$

where the variables have been defined previously.

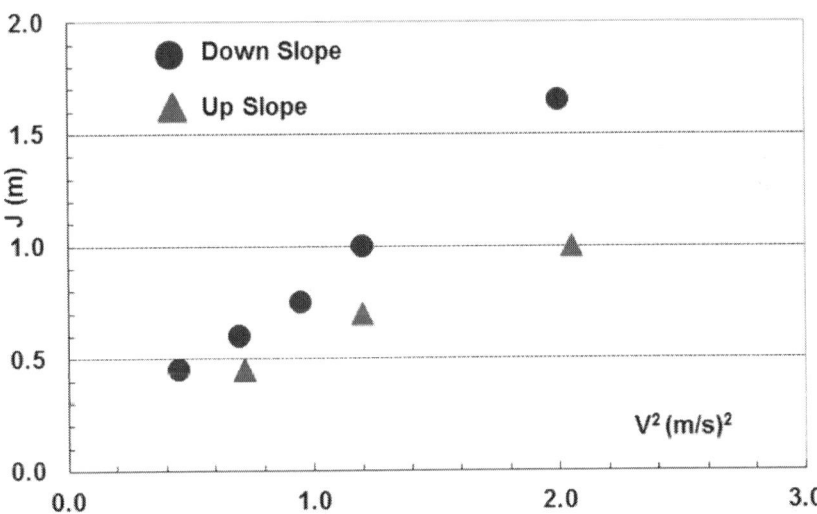

Figure 10 - Plot of distance run by balls against square of speed

The above chart shows that the results for either up slope or down slope are straight lines but there is a clear difference between up and down slope as expected.

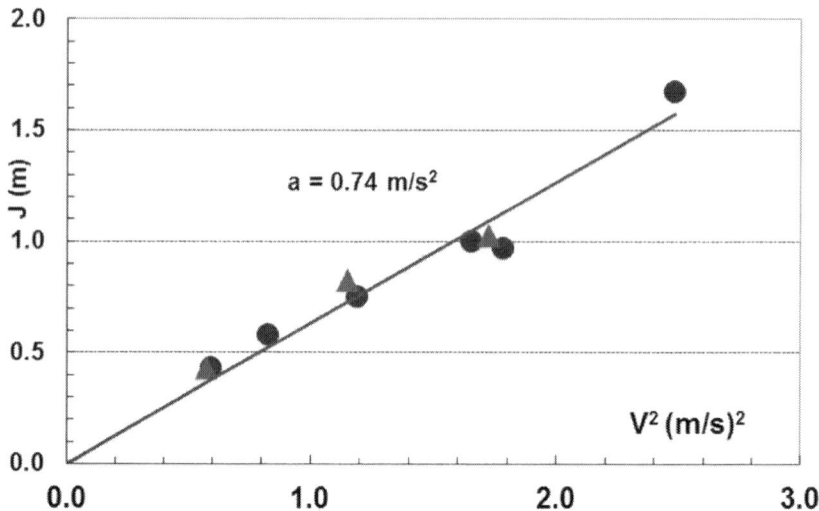

*Figure 11 - Plot of distance run by balls against square of speed*

However, when the results are corrected for the effect of gravity on balls rolling up or down a slope as in Figure 11 we see that the results for up and down slope fit together very well.

The derived deceleration '**a**' is 0.74 m/s² which compares with 0.65 m/s² for the carpet.

The green had been rained upon for about one hour just before the measurements following several days of dry weather. So, the green was wet but not saturated under foot.

Rather remarkably, the drag on this green was effectively the same whether it was wet or dry.

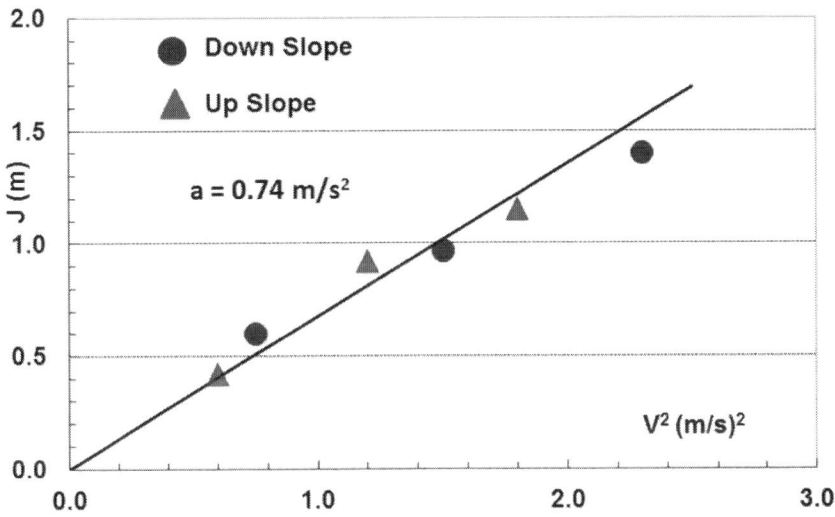

*Figure 12 - Results for the previous green when dry.*

This was confirmed (see Figure 12) following a long dry spell in the afternoon when the dew had evaporated. The value of '**a**' was measured again as 0.74 m/s².

However, on 7th May 2011 a measurement was made after two weeks without rain. The green tested was very hard and the ball bounced a lot when putted in the green.

The value for '**a**' was measured as 0.91 m/s².

| Condition | Drag Factor (a) m/s² |
|---|---|
| Short Pile Carpet | 0.65 |
| Very Wet Green | 0.74 |
| Dry, Recent Dew Green | 0.83 |
| Dry, Recent Dew Green | 0.74 |
| Dry Green | 0.80 |
| Parched, Hard and Bouncy Green | 0.91 |
| Parched, Hard and Bouncy Green | 0.87 |

*Table 1 - Comparisons of several drag measurements*

It seems that my living room carpet is a remarkably close simulation of a golf green both in the nature of the drag (independent of speed) and in value.

The curious feature in the above table is that dry greens appear to produce a higher drag on a ball than a wet green. This flies in the face of golf lore which says wet grass slows a ball down more and produces a 'slow' putting surface.

This was tested directly on my garden lawn which is about the same texture, when freshly mown, as the border of a green.

The ramp was used to roll balls along a flat part of the lawn which had not been rained upon for three weeks and so was hard and 'bouncy'. Over a period of several hours the area of lawn in use was then sprayed with water to the equivalent of 25 millimetres (one inch) of rain. The patch of lawn was then soft with the grass well wetted.

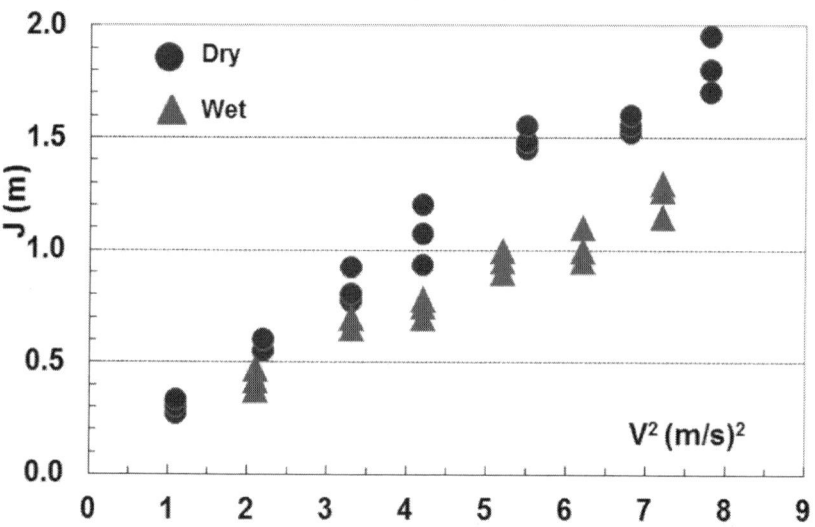

*Figure 13 - Comparison of wet and dry conditions on a simulated fairway.*

Figure 13 shows that wet fairway conditions produce higher drag than dry conditions which agrees with accepted golfing lore.

So, why is the reverse apparently true on greens?

The observation that the ball bounces quite a bit on hard, dry putting greens with little if any grass tufts to provide drag suggests that the drag should be lower under such conditions.

So, what's going on?

Are dry hard greens really 'faster' (low drag) or 'slower' (high drag)?

Does a bouncing ball on a hard green go further or less than a rolling ball on a softer more grassy green?

Whilst the measurement of drag indicates that dry hard greens have higher drag what does theory predict?

We will find an experimental and theoretical analysis of the effects of ball 'kicks' in Appendix B.

This same theory will also apply to fairways where, under dry conditions, a rolling ball is often observed to bounce in quite an animated fashion towards the green.

## 2.4 Coriolis Effect ($F_4$)

This causes the golf ball to swerve and occurs because the rotation of the Earth appears to make the putting green rotate under the ball as it travels in a straight line. To the observer being carried with the Earth, the ball appears to be curving.

The Coriolis Effect is well demonstrated by Foucault's Pendulum where a pendulum bob swings on a path that appears to slowly rotate as the Earth turns beneath it.

The effective rate at which the putting green turns beneath the rolling golf ball causes the ball to move on an arc of a circle with a radius of the order of 10 kilometres in temperate latitudes [11].

Clearly the Coriolis Effect has a minute effect on the path of a golf ball on a putting green. In fact, typically the ball is displaced by less than one millimetre even on long slow putts.

## 2.5 The initial skidding phase

Having established the forces acting on a rolling golf ball we will next consider the initial skidding phase.

When the ball is hit by the face of the putter it sets off with speed $V_H$ across the green. This report, as previously stated, does not claim to give advice about how to hit a ball at the right speed and along the right direction. That is far too complicated to include here and it has already been studied comprehensively in the literature. Here we start the analysis from the point that the ball leaves contact with the club head.

Initially the ball will not be rolling but skidding over the green.

# THE MATHEMATICS OF PUTTING

This is demonstrated by an excellent movie [12] on YouTube.

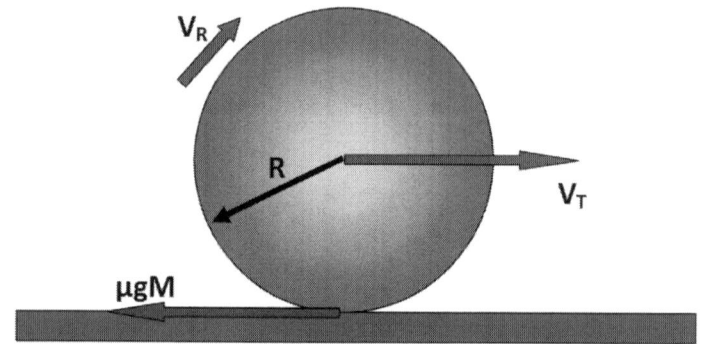

*Figure 14 - Dynamics of a skidding golf ball.*

The above diagram shows the dynamics of a skidding golf ball.

The speed of the ball across the green at any time after being hit and before the skidding phase ends is $V_T$. This is the translational speed.

The rotational speed, $V_R$ is initially zero but the ball rotation builds up until the two speeds - translational and rotational - match. At this point the ball stops skidding and is now rolling under the conditions described earlier.

The skidding force is shown as $\mu gM$ where $\mu$ is a dimensionless skidding friction coefficient. This force acts in two ways

1. The force speeds up the rotation of the ball. This increase in rotational kinetic energy draws from the translational kinetic energy and slows the ball down.

2. The skid force also draws kinetic energy from the ball and dissipates this as heat. This also slows the translational speed of the ball.

A set of measurements of the skidding phase of a putt have been made in which balls were illuminated by flashlights and photographed so that the rotational and translational speeds could be measured as the ball skidded across flat putting greens [13].

# THE MATHEMATICS OF PUTTING

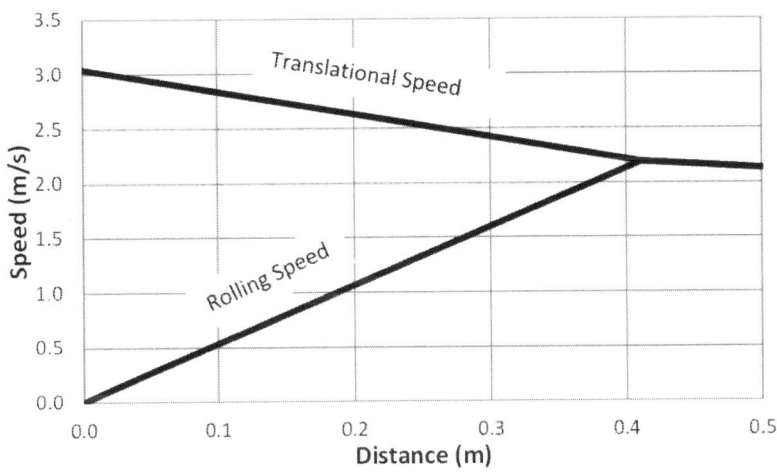

*Figure 15 - Measurements of ball skidding on a green*

Figure 15 above shows the results converted into metric units.

It can be seen how the rotational speed builds up at the expense of the translational speed until the two are the same. At this point the ball stops skidding and rolls. It is then subject to the rolling drag described in earlier pages and is seen as the downward sloping part of the chart on the right-hand side.

Before we can describe the mathematics of a skidding ball we need to have an estimate of **μ**.

*Figure 16 - Measurement of skid resistance*

# THE MATHEMATICS OF PUTTING

An experiment was set up, as shown in Figure 16, to measure $\mu$ for a sample of carpet which had already been shown to closely represent the characteristics of a medium speed green, see Table 1.

It took just 15 minutes to gather together the components, make the measurements and analyse the results.

A golf ball was dragged over a sample of carpet by a thread stuck to the ball. The thread was weighted by coins held in a cardboard tray and the weight needed to drag the ball at constant speed over the carpet sample was measured.

In the photograph above the three coins on the rear of the ball were placed there as a counterbalance to ensure that the attachment point of the thread to the ball was equal to the radius of the ball above the carpet sample.

From a set of trials the value of $\mu$ was measured at 0.52 meaning the skidding resistance is about one-half the gravitational force of the ball on the carpet sample.

Several other different carpet samples were tested but all gave a skid resistance factor $\mu$ in the region of 0.5

Correspondent Steve Eggleston has made similar measurements on real putting greens dragging a golf ball using a child's remote controlled car and a force gauge. This sounds like great fun but he no longer has the device and no pictures of it in action.

That's a shame.

His measurements appear to be very similar to mine with values of $\mu$ measured at around 0.5 being found on different types of green.

The equations governing a skidding golf ball can now be written.

The rotational speed on a flat green is given by

$$V_R = \frac{\mu g t}{\beta} \quad \text{(m/s)} \quad \text{(Equation 12)}$$

and the translational speed is given by the solution to the following equation

$$-\frac{dV_T}{dt} = \mu g + (\mu g)^2 \frac{t}{\beta V_T} \quad \text{(m/s}^2\text{)} \quad \text{(Equation 13)}$$

In the above two equations the symbols have meanings already defined but they are repeated here for convenience.

- β   Equal to 0.4
- μ   Skidding coefficient of drag
- g   Acceleration due to gravity, (9.81 m/s², 32 ft/s²)
- t   Time, sec
- $V_T$   Translational speed, m/s
- $V_R$   Rotational speed, m/s

An EXCEL™ model was produced to compute the skidding phase of a golf ball and results were produced using the value for μ measured with the golf ball dragged across a carpet sample.

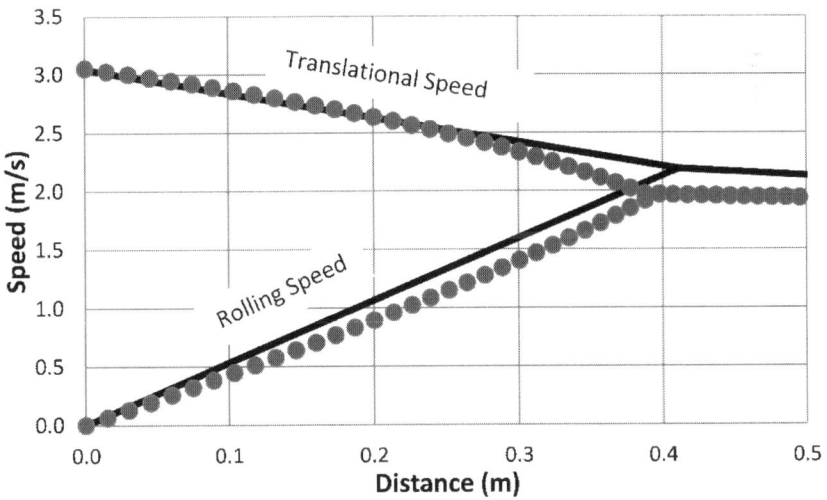

Figure 17 - Comparison of model with measurements for skidding golf ball.

It is a result like the one above that reminds me why I love science! A very simple experiment measures a physical value. This is plugged into a mathematical model and it agrees well with measurements.

The cynical reader will be stroking her chin and muttering

"Fudge!"

Sorry! That's exactly how it worked out for me.

No fudging.

# THE MATHEMATICS OF PUTTING

To be fair however, there must be an element of good luck here because we don't know the skid resistance of the green tested to obtain the full lines on the above figure.

But let's not quibble. It's clear that we have here a plausible mathematical model for a skidding golf ball on a level green.

Equations (12) and (13) have been solved numerically and the following relationships were found

The distance the ball travels in the skidding phase,

$$L_s = \frac{0.217 V_H^2}{\mu g} \quad \text{(Equation 14)}$$

The speed of the ball at the end of the skid,

$$V_s = 0.635 V_H \quad \text{(Equation 15)}$$

The time taken to reach the end of the skid,

$$T_s = \frac{0.257 V_H}{\mu g} \quad \text{(Equation 16)}$$

It is a simple matter to extend the above three equations to skidding over an inclined green. However, it has to be remembered in deriving the equations that the precessional turning for a skidding ball is a function of the rotational and translational speeds whereas, for a non-skidding ball, these two speeds are the same.

This makes the computation of the precessional turning of the ball whilst skidding a little more complicated on a sloping green.

Equation (4) has to be expanded to read

$$\frac{d\theta}{dt} = \frac{MgdR}{\beta MR^2 V_R + MR^2 V_T} = \frac{g\sin(I)\cos(\theta)}{\beta V_R + V_T} \quad \text{(Equation 17)}$$

At the start of the skidding part of a golf ball's journey the above equation becomes

$$\frac{d\theta}{dt} = \frac{g\sin(I)\cos(\theta)}{V_H} \quad \text{(Equation 18)}$$

where $V_H$ is the speed of the ball immediately after being hit.

At the end of the skid the rotational and translational speed are equal and equation (17) becomes

$$\frac{d\theta}{dt} = \frac{g\sin(I)\cos(\theta)}{0.635(1+\beta)V_H} \quad \text{(Equation 19)}$$

Because $\beta$ is equal to 0.4 it means that the rate of deviation of the ball down the slope of the green is 1.1 times greater at the end of the skid than at the start.

Thus, with reasonable accuracy we can represent the precessional turning of a golf ball as constant during the skidding phase and given by equation (18).

Applying equation (16) combined with equation (18) we get the change in direction of a golf ball over its skidding phase across a sloping green as

$$\frac{0.257\sin(I)\cos(\theta)}{\mu} \quad \text{(Equation 20)}$$

For a green sloping at 3 degrees (5.2%) this equation gives a change of direction equal to 1.5 degrees during the skidding phase.

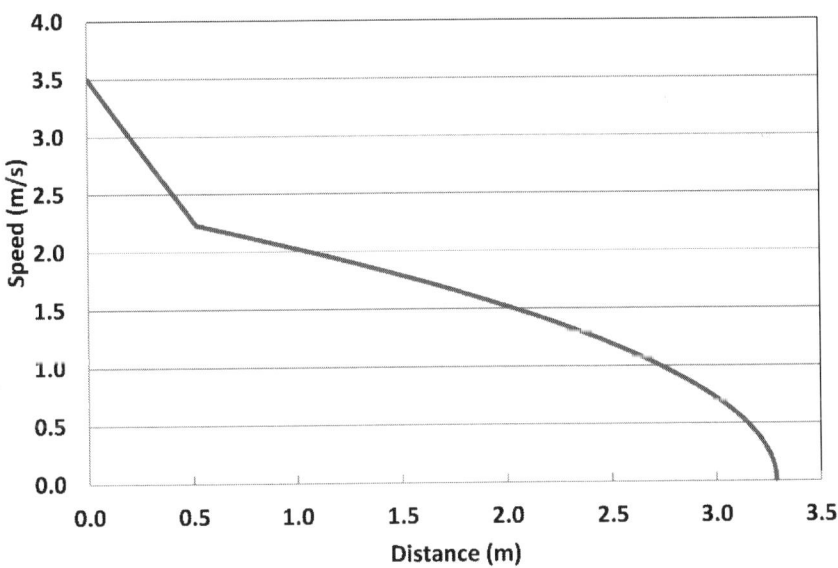

*Figure 18    A typical variation of ball speed over a green*

The above chart shows the speed of a golf ball after being hit across a typical green for a 3.3 metre (11 ft) putt. The effect of the initial skidding phase can clearly be seen.

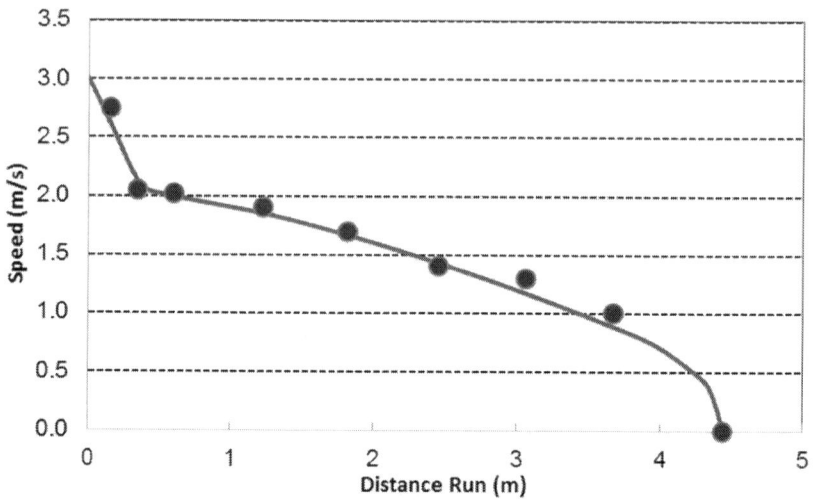

*Figure 19 - Comparison of experimental measurements with theory*

Figure 19 shows a comparison of measurements of a golf ball after being putted to a distance of about 4.4 metres on a plane short-tufted green [14].

The full curve is the solution of the equations (12) and (13) for the skidding phase and equation (7) for the free rolling phase.

The equations have been fitted to the measurements by assuming values of 0.70 for $\mu$ the skidding drag coefficient and 0.54 (m/s$^2$) for the rolling drag factor '**a**'.

A similar measurement on a short cropped carpet gave excellent agreement between measurement and theory when values of 0.29 was assumed for $\mu$ the skidding coefficient of drag and 0.62 for the rolling drag factor '**a**'. This latter value for 'a' is very close to my own measurements for a carpet which came out at 0.65 m/s$^2$.

The next part of this study describes the EXCEL™ model developed to visualise the above equations.

# 3. THE MATHEMATICAL MODEL AND ITS VALIDATION

We now have all the information needed to create a mathematical model for predicting the paths of golf balls rolling on inclined surfaces.

## 3.1 The Mathematical Model

The key equations taken from the previous chapter have been coded into an EXCEL ™ spreadsheet.

Skidding Phase

$$V_R = \frac{\mu g t}{\beta} \quad \text{(Equation 21)}$$

$$-\frac{dV_T}{dt} = \mu g + (\mu g)^2 \frac{t}{\beta V_T} \quad \text{(Equation 22)}$$

$$\frac{d\theta}{dt} = \frac{g \sin(I) \cos(\theta)}{\beta V_R + V_I} \quad \text{(Equation 23)}$$

Rolling Phase

$$\frac{d\theta}{dt} = \frac{g \sin(I) \cos(\theta)}{V(1+\beta)} \quad \text{(Equation 24)}$$

and

# THE MATHEMATICAL MODEL AND ITS VALIDATION

$$\frac{dV}{ds} = -\frac{g\sin(I)\sin(\theta)}{V(1+\beta)} - \frac{a}{V} \quad \text{(Equation 25)}$$

where we now know that '**a**' is a fixed value for a given surface.

In the above equations the symbols have meanings already defined but they are repeated here for convenience.

- $\beta$     Equal to 0.4
- $\mu$     Skidding coefficient of drag
- g     Acceleration due to gravity, (9.81 m/s², 32 ft/s²)
- s     Distance along the path of the ball's track
- t     Time, sec
- V     Speed of ball after skidding phase has ended
- $V_T$     Translational speed
- $V_R$     Rotational speed

The model was created in Microsoft™ EXCEL™. Inputting values for the following variables produced, by numerical integration, the path of the ball.

| Symbol | Variable | Units |
|---|---|---|
| $V_0$ | Initial Speed | m/s |
| $\theta_0$ | Initial Angle to Horizontal | degrees |
| a | Drag Factor | m/s² |
| $\beta$ | Inertia Factor | - |
| $\mu$ | Skidding friction coefficient | - |
| I | Inclination of Plane | Degrees |
| g | Acceleration due to Gravity | m/s² |

*Table 2 Mathematical Model Input Variables*

The figure below shows a typical graphical output.

# THE MATHEMATICAL MODEL AND ITS VALIDATION

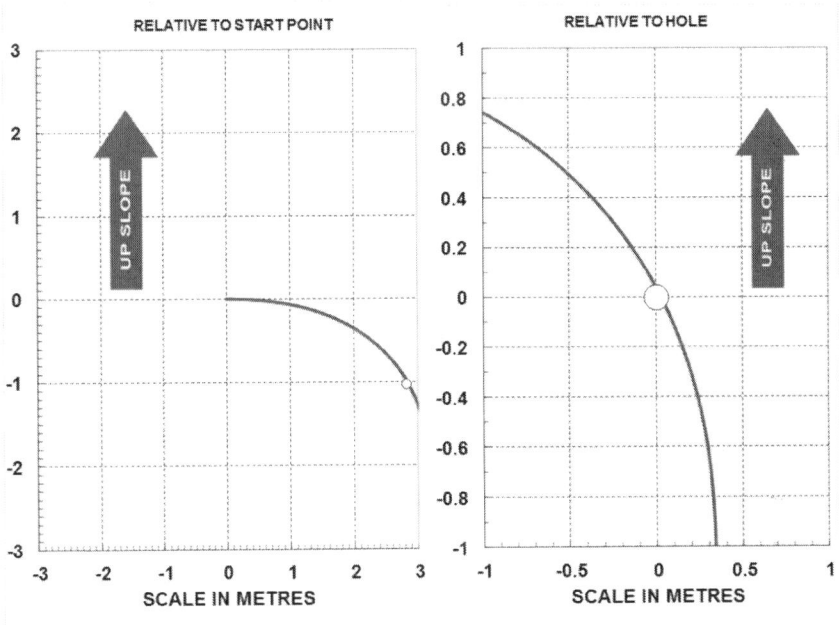

*Figure 20 - A typical result from the model.*

The model allows the predicted path of the ball to be plotted and the position of a cup can be input. If the centre of the ball is predicted to pass over the rim of the cup the displayed distance from the centre of the cup distance indicator changes colour as shown above. This shows that the ball potentially could drop into the cup.

In Chapter 5 the circumstances under which a golf ball either drops into the cup, rolls around the rim or bounces out will be modelled. However, for this Chapter only the track of the ball is computed.

# THE MATHEMATICAL MODEL AND ITS VALIDATION

It is important to validate this mathematical model against measurements of a ball moving on an inclined plane - and this will be described next.

## 3.2 Model validation against experiment

The skidding part of the ball's path has already been validated so I set up an experiment to measure the path of golf balls rolling over an inclined plane to verify the rolling phase of the model.

*Figure 21 - Experimental set up using a piece of living room carpet as a simulation*

The experimental arrangement consisted of a rectangle of living room carpet mounted on a rigid wooden board which could be tilted. In the above picture the board is raised at the far side nearest to me.

Golf balls were rolled down a ramp and across the carpet sample. These set off across the carpet parallel to the horizontal ($\theta_o$ = 0 degrees) and then they curved down the slope.

The stopping points of the balls were plotted using a marker pen so that the end of the paths could be compared with model predictions.

Unfortunately, this arrangement did not work well because the carpet sample was smaller than desired. My wife had - with some

## THE MATHEMATICAL MODEL AND ITS VALIDATION

justification perhaps - been loathe to let me cut a rectangle out of our living room carpet of adequate size; her criterion being that the hole in the living room carpet must be covered by a chair.

The possibility of returning the rectangle of carpet to its hole after the experiment was complete was unreasonable because it had, by then, been covered in marker pen data points.

The experiment was redesigned so that the bare wooden board was covered with a large sheet of paper marked in 50 millimetre squares.

This had the advantage that the drag of the surface on the ball was small so that the prediction of the balls' paths should be easier to make and more accurate.

A large number of tests were conducted using different ramp slope angles, board inclinations and starting distances on the ramps.

*Figure 22 - View of the experiment in its final form*

After experimenting with covering the paper with icing sugar and cooking flour to make the ball tracks visible, the solution was found to roll the ball after making it damp. This left a track of small wet patches which were quickly marked on the paper and annotated before they dried out.

On Figures 23 and 24 the starting points and paths of the balls are marked by arrows.

# THE MATHEMATICAL MODEL AND ITS VALIDATION

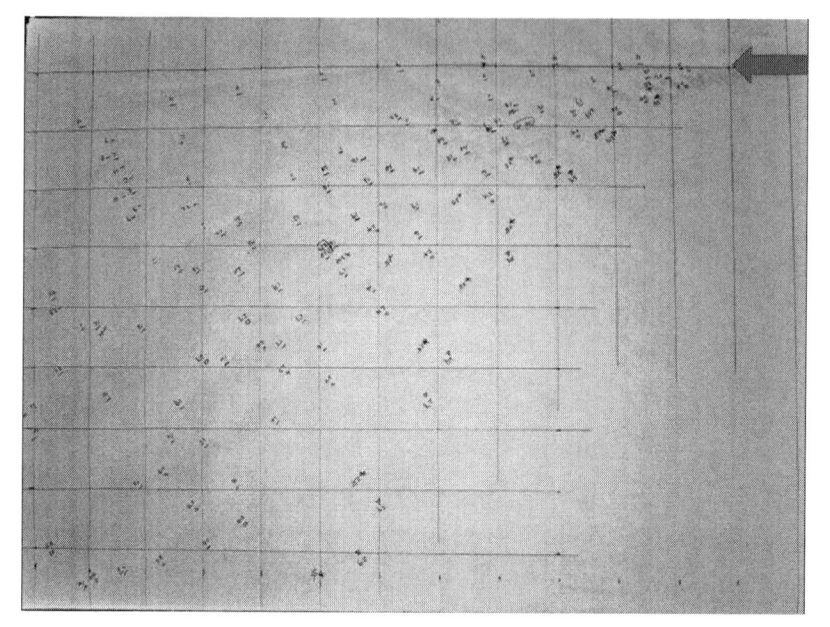

*Figure 23 - The tracks marked on the paper covering the inclined plane*

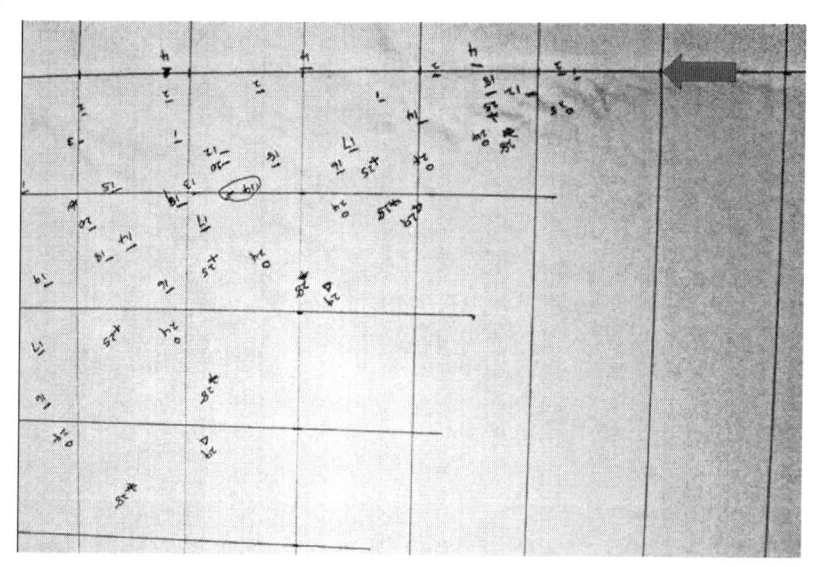

*Figure 24 - Close-up of the tracks marked on the paper covering the inclined plane*

These tracks were carefully measured and the positions of the ball compared with the mathematical solution of the equations derived earlier.

# THE MATHEMATICAL MODEL AND ITS VALIDATION

Although the drag on the rolling golf ball was small on the solid wooden board it is necessary to measure the value so that the model can be rigorously test.

Accordingly, the experimental arrangement shown below was set up.

*Figure 25 - Measurement of drag on the board*

The board was tilted at an angle $A_2$ to the horizontal and a golf ball was rolled down a ramp tilted at angle $A_1$. The geometry of the ramp was kept constant but the tilt of the board was varied. The distance the ball rolled up the board before stopping and rolling back down was carefully marked.

Let us assume that the ball arrives at the end of the ramp at a constant speed $U_0$. Its speed as it starts up the board is

$U_1 = U_0 \cos(A_1 + A_2)$  (Equation 26)

The distance travelled up the board (**L***) is then given by

$$\frac{\cos^2(A_1 + A_2)}{L^*} = \frac{2(g \sin(A_2) + a)}{U_1^2 (1 + \beta)}$$  (Equation 27)

If we plot the left-hand group of variables against $\sin(A_2)$ then we should end up with data points along a straight line.

The ratio of the intercept to the gradient will be **a/g**.

## THE MATHEMATICAL MODEL AND ITS VALIDATION

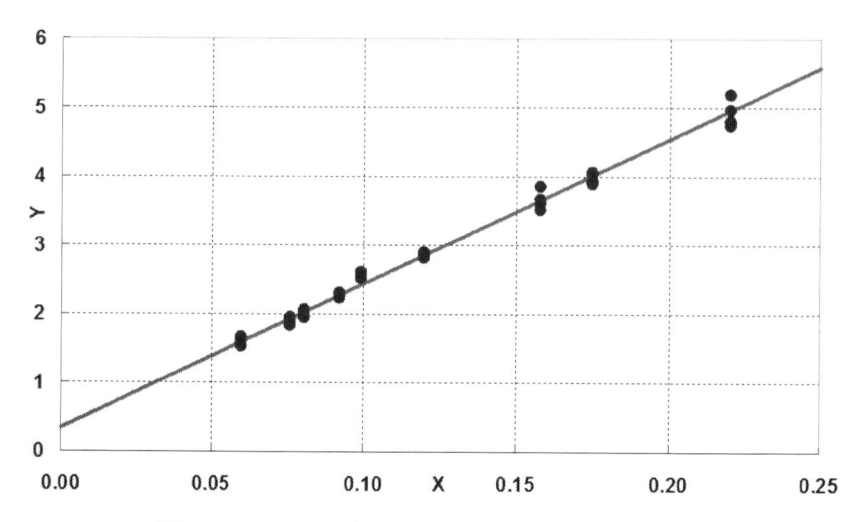

*Figure 26 - Derivation of drag on the board*

The figure above shows the result from this experiment.

It can be seen that the data do indeed fall on a straight line and, in consequence, we find that

**a** = 0.16 m/s²    Equation (28)

for the surface of the board.

We now have all the information we need to test the model against measured golf ball trajectories on an inclined plane.

Before showing the results we can make a substantial simplification in the analysis.

The path of the ball can be expressed in terms of dimensionless distances across and down the slope as follows

$$X' = \frac{x \, g \, \sin(I)}{U_1^2} \quad \text{Equation (29)}$$

$$Y' = \frac{y \, g \, \sin(I)}{U_1^2} \quad \text{Equation (30)}$$

where **x** is the actual distance travelled across the slope, **y** is the distance travelled down the slope, **g** is the acceleration due to gravity (9.81 m/s²), **I** is the inclination of the slope, $U_1$ is the speed of the ball as it sets off across the board and **X'**, **Y'** are the dimensionless values of **x** and **y**.

## THE MATHEMATICAL MODEL AND ITS VALIDATION

The chart below shows the results.

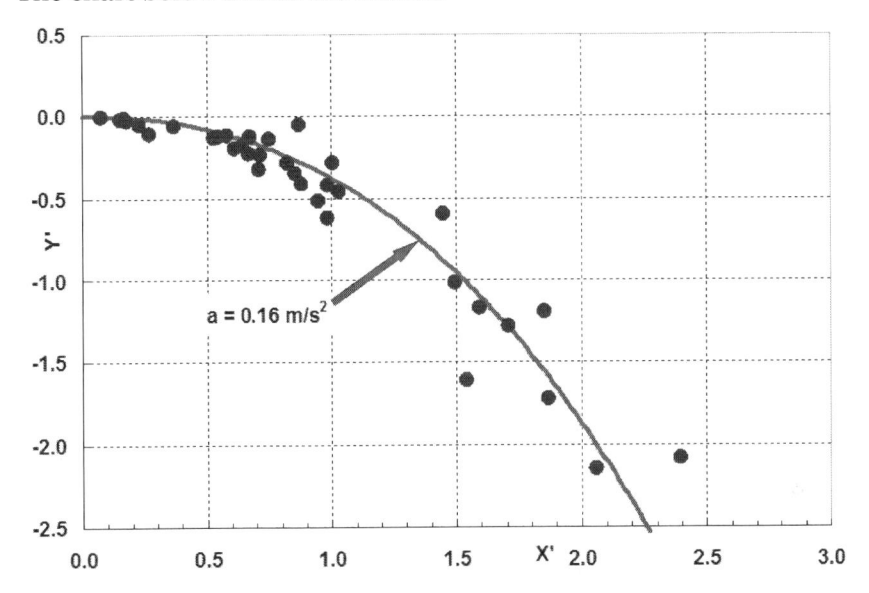

*Figure 27 - Comparison of measurements with model.*

We see from this plot that the measurements of golf ball trajectories on a smooth, low drag inclined plain give an excellent agreement with theory.

We now have a validated mathematical model of a golf ball rolling on an inclined plane.

Before moving on to use this model to investigate the trajectories of golf balls on putting surfaces we will divert off at a small tangent partially because the Stimpmeter is a very important, but misunderstood, piece of golfing equipment and also because it will allow the reader's brain to cool down after all the preceding analysis.

# THE MATHEMATICAL MODEL AND ITS VALIDATION

*Figure 28 - It's handy to have the first one hundred digits of $\pi$ close by.*

# 4 THE 'STIMPMETER'

After about one year of making extensive measurements using balls rolling down ramps I saw a very similar device in use at St Andrew's Golf Course during a television programme.

I was fascinated and replayed that short element of the televised event several times.

Subsequently I did a search of the web and 'discovered' the Stimpmeter [15].

This was invented in the 1930s and these devices have been widely used for decades for measuring the 'speed' of greens [15].

And I had thought I had invented an original device!

Oh well! There's no point now in me trying to take out a patent on the use of ramps to measure green drag!

The Stimpmeter consists of a metal V-shaped channel with a notch near one end. The ball is sat on the channel held in position by the notch. As the channel is lifted, an angle is reached (about 20 degrees) at which the ball is no longer held by the notch. The ball rolls down the channel and across the golf green. The distance travelled (in feet) is the rating of that green.

# THE STIMPMETER

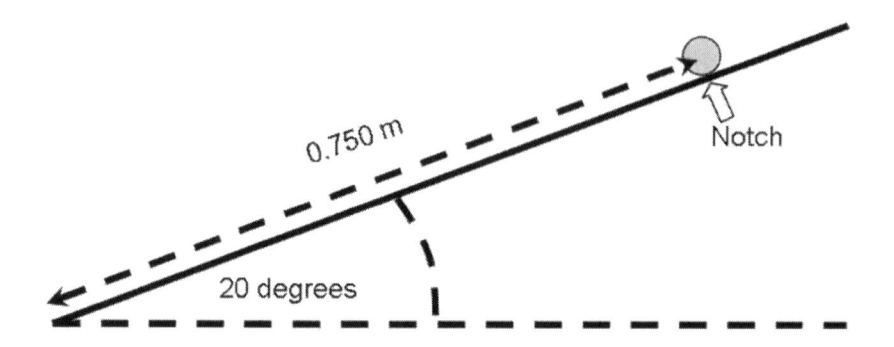

*Figure 29 - The dimensions of a Stimpmeter at the angle of ball release*

We can use the dimensions on the above diagram together with the equation

$$V^2 = \frac{2\,g\,0.75\sin(20°)\cos^2(20°)}{1+\beta} = 2\,J\,a \quad \text{(Equation 31)}$$

to work out the effective values for '**a**' and these are shown in the table below.

The ball sets off across the green from a Stimpmeter with speed 1.8 m/s (5.9 ft/sec).

For the standard USGA Stimpmeter the drag parameter '**a**' can be computed by using a simple equation where **J** is the distance rolled from the Stimpmeter.

$$a = 1.6\,/\,J \quad \text{(Equation 32)}$$

USGA Stimpmeter measurements on a huge number of putting greens across the USA produced the following classifications [16]

# THE STIMPMETER

| | USGA Standard J | a (m/s²) | US Open J | a (m/s²) |
|---|---|---|---|---|
| Slow greens | 1.0 (ft) / 0.30 (m) | 5.29 | 6.5 (ft) / 1.98 (m) | 0.81 |
| Medium Greens | 4.5 (ft) / 1.37 (m) | 1.18 | 8.5 (ft) / 1.58 (m) | 0.62 |
| Fast Greens | 6.5 (ft) / 1.98 (m) | 0.81 | 10.5 (ft) / 3.19 (m) | 0.50 |
| High USGA Limit | - | - | 15.0 (ft) / 4.56 (m) | 0.35 |

*Table 3 - Table of Stimpmeter measurements with computed values for drag '**a**'*

My own measurements of '**a**' range from 0.74 to 0.91 m/s² which are well inside the above range for medium and fast Standard USGA greens.

Douglas Breede developed a formula for use on sloping greens [17] which is

$$\text{Corrected Speed} = \frac{2 J_U J_D}{J_U + J_D} = J_0 \quad \text{(Equation 33)}$$

This gives the equivalent distance travelled on a flat green when measurements can only be made up and down a slope.

However, with our knowledge of how golf balls run on inclined surfaces - at least when going directly up or down the slope, we can test this equation.

Imagine a ball setting off at speed **V** from a Stimpmeter both up and then down the slope.

The distances up and down slope are given by

$$J_U = \frac{V^2}{2\left(a + \frac{g\sin(I)}{(1+\beta)}\right)} \quad \text{(Equation 34)}$$

$$J_D = \frac{V^2}{2\left(a - \frac{g\sin(I)}{(1+\beta)}\right)} \quad \text{(Equation 35)}$$

Hence, with a little algebra, we find that Brede's formula for sloping greens gives the corrected 'speed' as

# THE STIMPMETER

$$\text{Corrected Green 'Speed'} = J_0 = \frac{V^2}{2a} = \frac{1.6}{a} \text{(metres)} = \frac{5.25}{a} \text{(ft)}$$

(Equation 36)

which is precisely the distance the ball would be travelled on a flat green.

So, Brede's equation is consistent with the model presented here.

There are minor issues with the Stimpmeter.

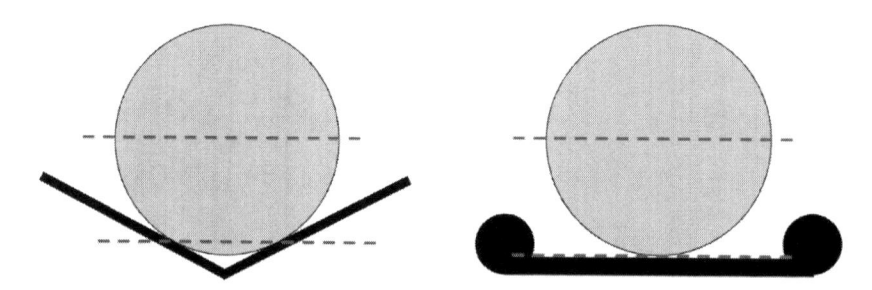

*Figure 30 - Profile of Stimpmeter channel (left) and ramp that I use (right).*

Figure 30 above shows the profile of my ramp compared with the Stimpmeter's 'V' shaped channel. The latter is an angled trough with an included angle of 145 degrees. The golf ball makes contact above the base of the ball as indicated by the dashed line. This means that the spin of the ball is faster than if it had rolled down a flat plane.

The effect is that more potential energy is diverted into spinning the ball and, in consequence, the ball's speed at the end of the ramp is slower than it would have been on a flat ramp.

In contrast, the right-hand diagram shows the ramp that I use. The edges are solely there to guide the ball down the ramp.

What this means is that the value for $\beta$ for my ramp is the theoretical value of 0.4 whereas for the Stimpmeter $\beta$ is 0.42 making any direct comparison between results from my ramp and the standard Stimpmeter slightly uncertain. This is because the ball will leave the Stimpmeter slower than from my ramp.

However, once the ball is on the green the excess rotational energy is quickly converted back into kinetic energy so that the ball will 'leap forward' and settle quickly down to roll at the same speed as

## THE STIMPMETER

from my ramp under the same conditions.

Another problem is that the angle of 20 degrees at which the ball releases itself from the notch may not be repeatable and, indeed, various researchers quote the release angle as 20 degrees, 20.5 degrees and even 22 degrees.

However, it is a requirement of using measurements from a Stimpmeter that three consecutive balls must lie within 8 inches (0.200 m) as defined by the USGA instruction manual for the Stimpmeter.

Table 3 shows large variations in 'green speeds' that can be encountered (from 0.3 to 4.5 metres, 1 ft to 15 ft) so such considerations are probably trivial in day-to-day golf green maintenance.

*Figure 31 - A wooden ramp used instead of a Stimpmeter.*

I made a ramp, as shown above, which costs practically nothing and can be used by anyone to measure green speeds and inclination angles.

A length of dado rail about 0.8 metres in length had a matchstick glued at 0.75 metres from the lower. This held a golf ball so that the ball was released when the ramp was raised to 20 degrees.

# THE STIMPMETER

The height of the ridge holding the ball must be 1.3 millimetres high. The fine adjustment was made by sticking sheets of thin card (shown black above) until the ball released at the correct angle.

This device was made entirely from material found unwanted in my garage.

# 5 HOLING THE BALL

Figure 32 shows a ball with radius **R** travelling at speed $V_H$ heading towards the mouth of a cup accurately across its centre.

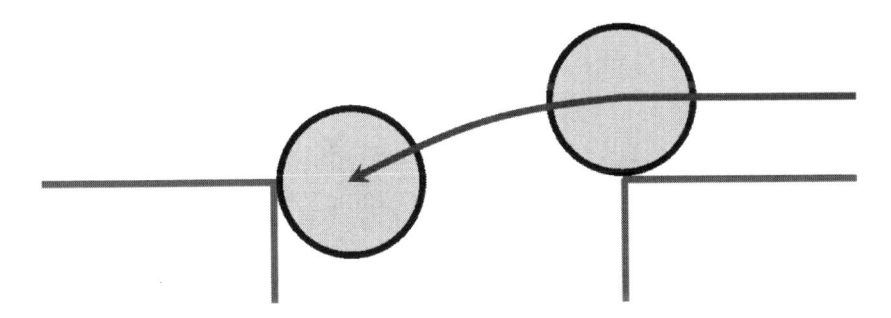

*Figure 32 - Geometry of ball rolling into a cup drawn to scale*

As the ball flies across the mouth of the hole it drops under gravity and either it hits the opposite lip, inner wall or drops into the cup.

If the ball hits the inner wall it bounces into the cup. In this case the distance dropped under gravity on hitting the opposite rim of the cup will have exceeded the radius of the ball and the ball will be holed.

The limit is when the ball has dropped under gravity by its radius as shown above.

Thus the ball will drop into the hole if

## HOLING THE BALL

$$R < \frac{1}{2}gT^2 = \frac{1}{2}g\left(\frac{D-R}{V_H}\right)^2 \quad \text{(Equation 37)}$$

where **T** is the time taken for the front of the ball to travel to the far side of the hole and **D** is the diameter of the cup.

Hence, the highest speed at which the ball will certainly drop into the hole is given by

$$V_H = \left(\frac{D}{R} - 1\right)\sqrt{\frac{gR}{2}} \quad \text{(Equation 38)}$$

We know that **D** is 0.108 metres, the radius of the ball **R** is 0.021 metres and **g** is 9.81 m/s² (32 ft/s²)

This gives a speed of 1.3 m/s (4.3 ft/s). If the ball reaches the hole heading for the centre with this speed or slower it will drop into the cup.

John Zumerchik quotes a figure of 4.6 ft/s (1.4 m/s) [18] although he does not show where this figure comes from.

Holmes [19] quotes a figure of 1.31 m/s which is very close to my figure.

This result is independent of the state of the green. It is a fundamental speed for holing a golf ball.

If the ball hits the far side rim rather than the inner wall of the cup it will bounce off the rim and either

a. drop back into the cup,

b. bounce back over the cup to land on the green, or

c. bounce forwards to land on the green.

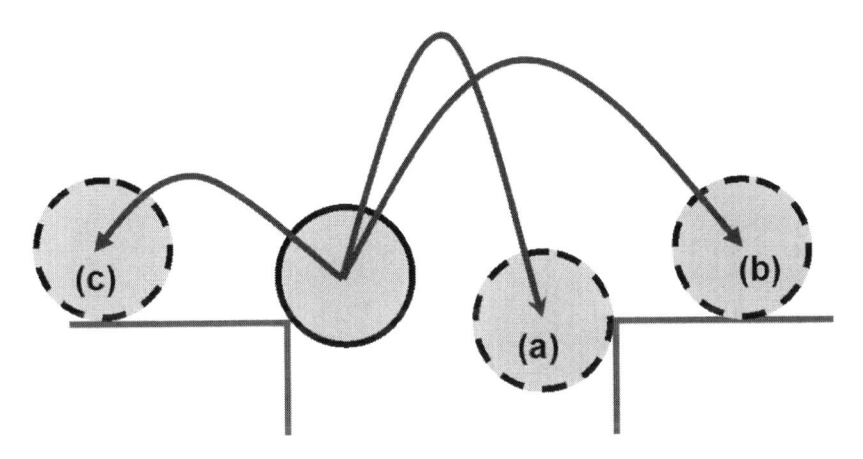

*Figure 33 - A ball which bounces off the rim can go any one of three ways*

The path of the ball after hitting the far side of the rim centrally is determined by two factors; the speed at which the ball approaches the hole and the Coefficient Of Restitution (COR) denoted by ε [20]. This is the ratio of the ball speed before and after hitting the grass surface. It is a measure of the rigidity or 'bounciness' of the surface.

It is simple to measure.

Drop a ball from any height $H_1$ and measure how high it bounces, $H_2$. The COR is given by

$$\varepsilon = \sqrt{\frac{H_2}{H_1}} \quad \text{(Equation 39)}$$

This follows because the speed on impact from height $H_1$ is proportional to the square-root of $H_1$ and ε is defined as the ratio of speeds before and after impact.

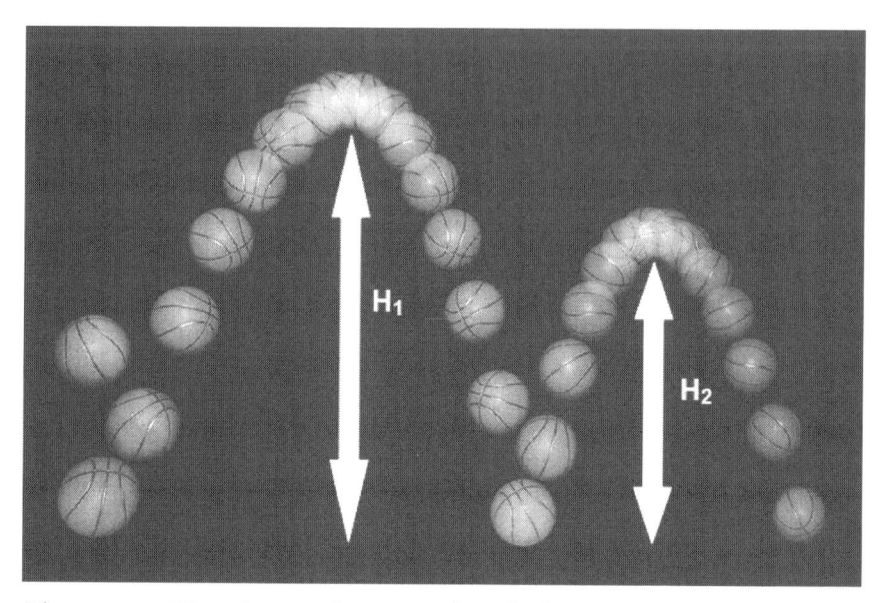

*Figure 34 - Time lapse photographs of a bouncing ball [21].*

Typical values measured by dropping a golf ball and measuring the rebounds are

| Surface | COR | Surface | COR |
|---|---|---|---|
| Tile kitchen floor | 0.82 | Plank of wood | 0.48 |
| Dry golf green | 0.40 | Damp golf green | 0.38 |
| Thin carpet tiles | 0.34 | Living room carpet | 0.20 |

*Table 4 - Typical Coefficient Of Restitution values*

The path of the ball after hitting the rim of the cup, as shown diagrammatically in Figure 33, can be computed and Figure 35 below shows the conditions under which the ball will either drop into the cup, bounce into the cup or bounce out and land outside the cup.

# HOLING THE BALL

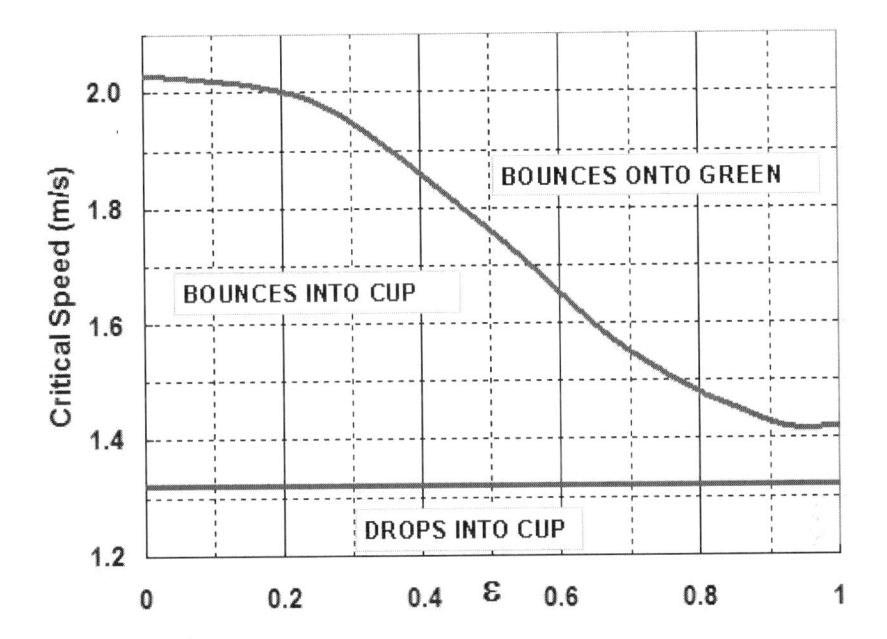

*Figure 35 - Conditions under which a golf ball is holed in a central approach.*

For the purpose of mathematical modelling it was found that the upper curve can be closely represented empirically by the equation

$$V_C = 2.03 - 1.24\,\varepsilon^2 + 0.63\,\varepsilon^4 \quad \text{(Equation 40)}$$

A simple contraption was made to test the dynamics of getting a golf ball into a hole and to test the theoretical curve in the above chart. This is shown below.

This consisted of a ramp to roll a golf ball towards a hole in a thick plank of wood.

The result of any ball roll was noted in terms of the three outcomes on Figure 35 above as a function of the speed of the ball and the aim point relative to the centre of the hole.

# HOLING THE BALL

*Figure 36 - Overall view of the ramp and artificial golf hole*

*Figure 37 - View of the ramp and the sophisticated (?) method of adjusting the slope*

# HOLING THE BALL

*Figure 38 - Another view of the ramp*

*Figure 39 - Ball's eye view of the ramp and artificial hole*

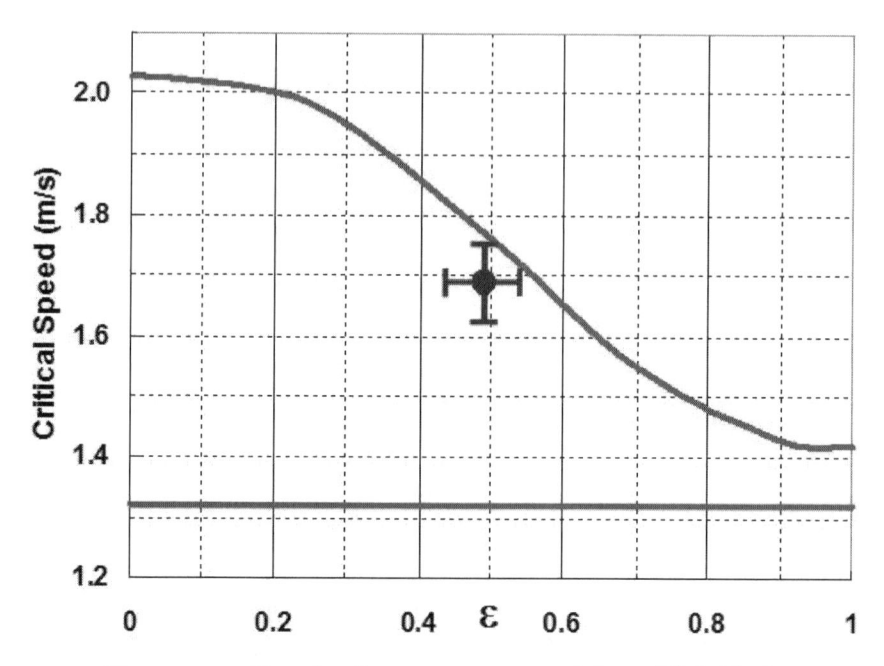

*Figure 40 - Result of measurement with artificial hole*

For balls aimed at the centre of the hole the critical speed was measured as 1.69 m/s. The Coefficient of Restitution was found to be 0.48 by bouncing a golf ball repeatedly off the plank from different heights. This gives a good agreement with the computed curve on Figure 40 bearing in mind the inherent difficulty of making the measurements.

If the ball runs towards the hole but not on the central line it will be given an impulse towards the centre of the hole and hit the lip at a speed and position that is very complicated to calculate. In general, the lip of the hole will push the ball so that it rides on the lip and runs off at an angle from the original direction.

This is observed with the artificial hole as in real life.

HOLING THE BALL

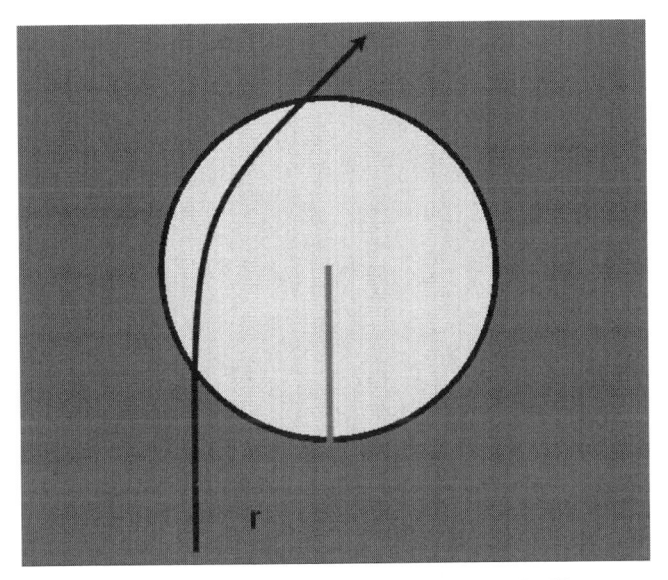

*Figure 41 - Path of an off centre ball*

*Figure 42 - Experimental investigation into the critical speed for off-centre shots.*

The device used to determine the critical speed for holing a golf ball was used to investigate the critical speed for balls which arrive at the hole off centre as shown above.

It was found that the critical speed decreases with distance offset from the hole centre as shown below.

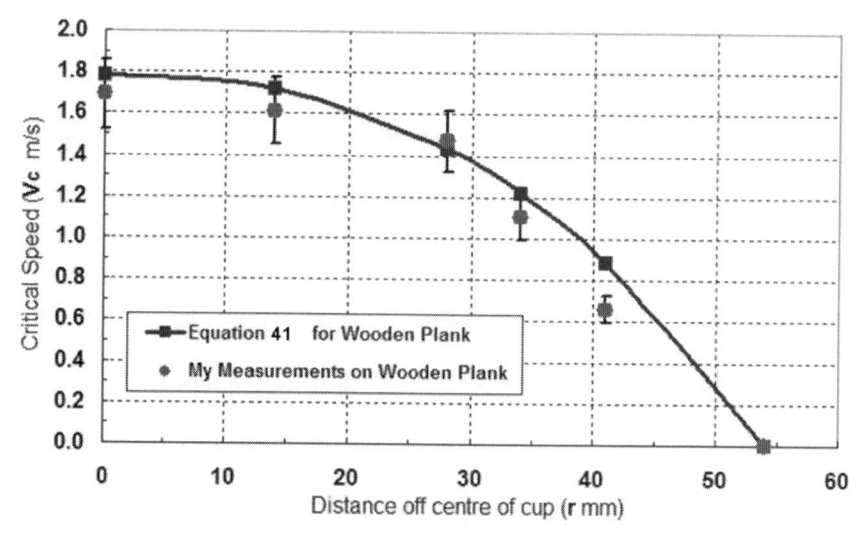

*Figure 43 - Critical holing speed for off centre shots, $\varepsilon = 0.48$*

The continuous curve is my empirical fit to the data points given by

$$V_c = \left(2.03 - 1.24\,\varepsilon^2 + 0.63\,\varepsilon^4\right)\left(1 - \left|\frac{r}{54}\right|^{2.5}\right) \quad r < 54 \text{ mm (m/s)}$$

(Equation 41)

where $V_c$ is the critical maximum ball speed to drop into the hole (m/s) computed by equation (39) for the central path corrected for the off-centre distance, $\varepsilon$ is the Coefficient Of Restitution (COR) and $r$ is the distance of the ball path from the hole centre (mm)

An experimental and theoretical study of the conditions under which a golf ball will drop into a cup was carried out by Holmes [22] on real putting greens.

He derived the empirical equation

$$V_c = 1.63\left(1 - \left|\frac{r}{54}\right|^2\right) \text{ (m/s)} \quad \text{(Equation 42)}$$

No variation in the on-centre critical speed was apparently considered to account for varying grass conditions. The figure of 1.63 m/s corresponds to a Coefficient of Restitution of about 0.61 which is slightly higher than values around 0.5 which are typical of my measurements.

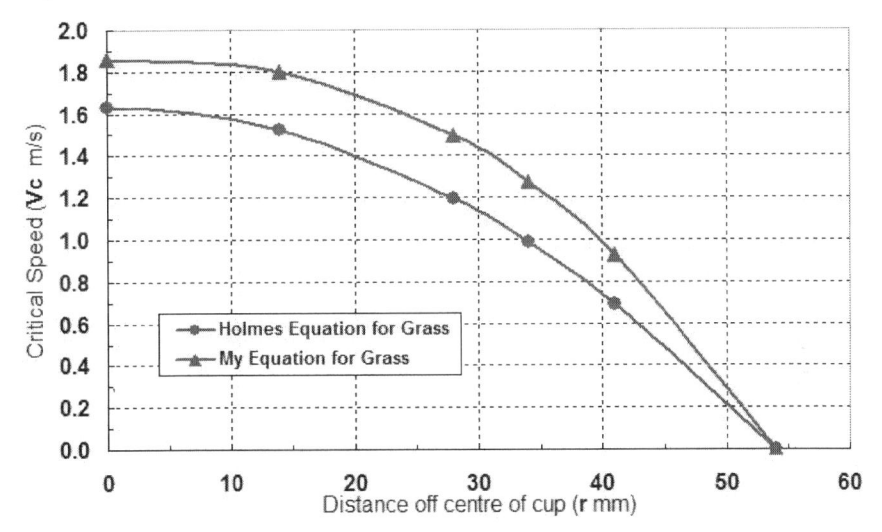

*Figure 44 - Critical holing speed for off centre shots for a grass green*

If we accept the generalised equation (41) as representative of real green conditions then we now have all the validated equations needed to compute the path of a golf ball across a perfect inclined plane and decide whether or not it will end up in a cup, will bounce off the rim back onto the green or roll past the cup.

Before revealing this mathematical model and showing predictions made using it we must firstly understand the nature of randomness on the putting green and what the difference is between luck, skill and mathematical precision.

# HOLING THE BALL

# 6. RANDOMNESS, SKILL AND MATHEMATICAL MODELLING

No putting shot is ever perfect.

A putt will be imperfect for three main reasons.

a. There are imperfections in the surface of the green that cause random deviations in the path of the ball; for example, small divots, indentations caused by balls landing on the green from chip shots, leaves, worm casts, unexpected gusts of wind, etc.

b. The golfer does not hit the ball at the correct speed, and

c. The golfer does not hit the ball in the correct direction.

All three of these causes for a ball going astray are random. The first is due to randomness in nature and the last two are randomness in the golfer.

Little can be done about the first cause of error. Years of practice can reduce, but not eliminate, causes (b) and (c).

The natural sources of random deviation in the path of a ball over a green (the first item in the above list) are many. Any golfer who has attempted a long putt will be all too aware of the way the ball bounces, swerves this way and that finally making that frustrating final veer away from the lip of the cup at the last moment.

This is going to require a short excursion into the world of 'Statistics' and we must pause for a while to explain what is meant by the terms Standard Deviation ($\sigma$) and Mean ($\mu$).

If a process involves the combination of a large number of random variables then the overall probability distribution (the 'spread') tends towards what is called the 'Gaussian' [23], Normal' or 'Bell' distribution. This is a consequence of the 'Central Limit Theorem'; one of the most powerful theorems in mathematics. We are not going to delve into the Central Limit Theorem here - this isn't necessary for what follows and there are excellent explanations that can be followed up if required [24] [25].

As an illustration of the Central Limit Theory, I hit a golf ball one hundred times towards a marker.

I measured the position of the ball each time and the scatter of the balls is plotted below.

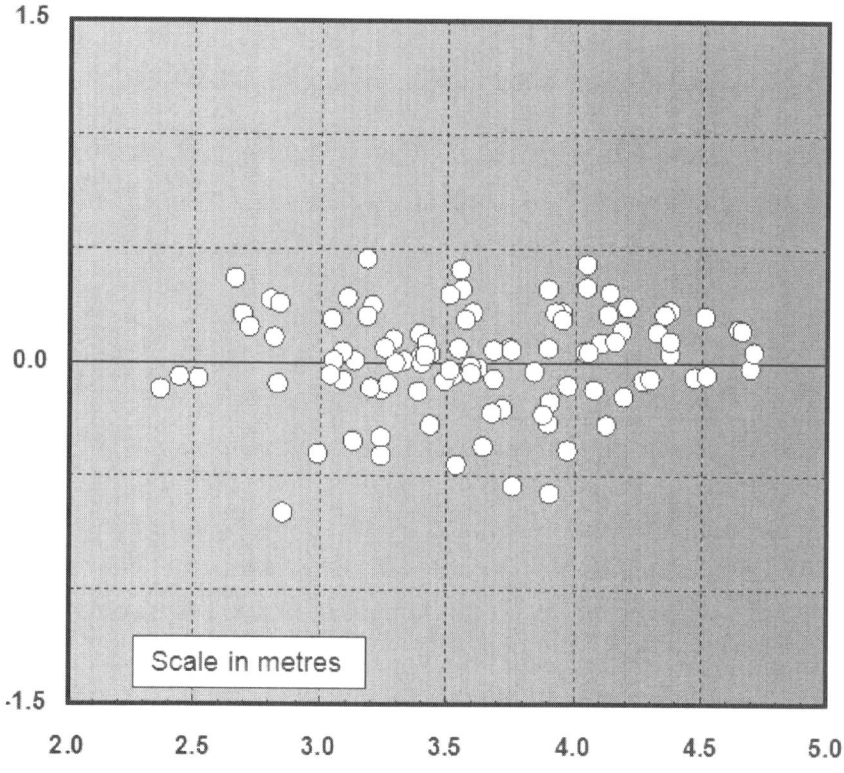

*Figure 45 - Scatter diagram for one hundred balls hit on a flat putting green.*

The ball was initially hit from the origin of the graph 2 metres off the left of the chart.

The scatter in the end position of the ball can be considered as due to a random scatter in range and a random scatter in angle; the latter creating the cross-track scatter.

# RANDOMNESS, SKILL AND MATHEMATICAL MODELLING

For now just concentrate on the scatter in range which we see extends from 2.4 metres (7.9 ft) out to 4.7 metres (15.4 ft).

The scatter can be defined by two numbers - the 'Mean' ($\mu$) and the 'Standard Deviation' ($\sigma$).

The mean is the average of the along-range values and defines the centre of the scatter.

The Standard Deviation ($\sigma$) defines the spread of the scatter about the Mean ($\mu$).

Figure 45 below shows a plot of the proportion of balls for which the range is less than a stated value. These are the plotted data points.

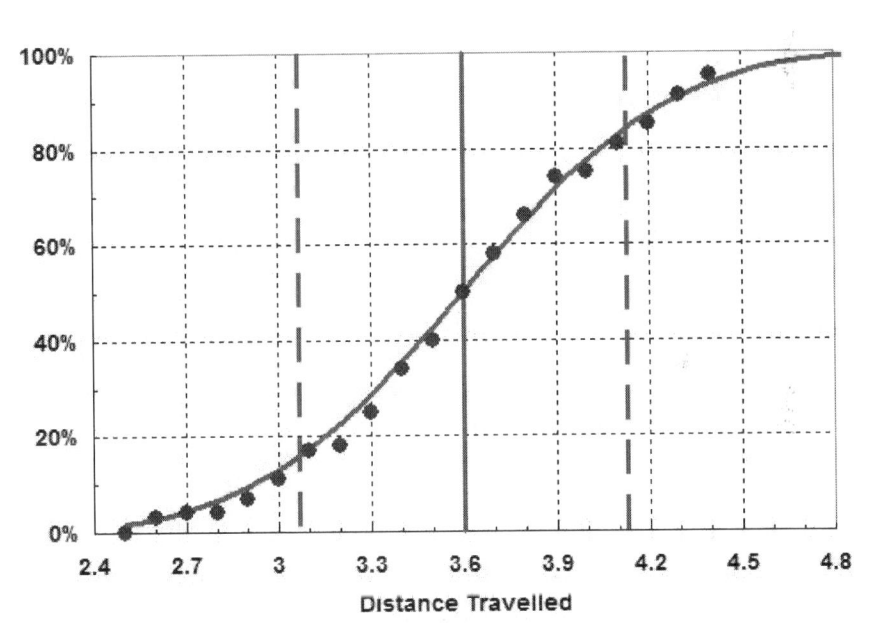

*Figure 46 - Comparison of 100 ball shots with the Gaussian Distribution*

If we assume that the scatter follows a 'Gaussian' probability distribution then the proportion of balls predicted to lie out to range '**x**' is given by

$$\text{Prob} = \frac{1}{\sigma\sqrt{2}} \int_{-\infty}^{x} e^{-(t-\mu)^2/2\sigma^2} dt \quad \text{(Equation 43)}$$

# RANDOMNESS, SKILL AND MATHEMATICAL MODELLING

This equation has been solved for values of σ equal to 0.53 metres (1.7 ft) and μ equal to 3.6 metres (12 ft). This is the full curve in the graph above.

We can see that equation (43) represents the experimental points rather well.

The continuous vertical line marks μ for the data points and the green vertical lines show the upper and lower values for σ relative to μ.

It is the characteristic of the 'Gaussian' distribution that 68% of data points lie within ± σ of the mean. This is an easy way to determine the value of σ.

At this point professional statisticians will be rolling their eyes and gnashing their teeth because σ is actually determined by the equation [26]

$$\sigma = \sqrt{\frac{1}{n-1}\sum_{i=1}^{n}(x_i - \mu)^2} \quad \text{(Equation 44)}$$

where 'n' is the sample size, $x_i$ is the individual sample and μ is the mean.

However, the rule of thumb that 68% of data points lie with ± σ of the mean is good enough for golfers.

It is also not rigorous but, for our purposes, acceptable to assume that the Mean is equal to the Median; this latter being the value on the horizontal axis of Figure 45 where the probability equals 50%.

We now return to the random natural errors encountered on a putting green.

These natural random variations have been investigated experimentally by Frank Werner and Richard Grieg who used a mechanical putting machine to send balls off on a variety of greens at a carefully controlled speed and direction [27] and noted the variation in the stopping positions of the balls on the greens.

The Standard Deviation (σ) was found to be 1.1 degrees in angular direction and 2% in range.

At 2.7 metres (8.9 ft) range the radius of the standard golf cup subtends an angle of 1.1 degrees. Because this is the Standard Deviation of the angular deviation imposed by the green surface

# RANDOMNESS, SKILL AND MATHEMATICAL MODELLING

irregularities it follows that at a range of 2.7 metres (8.9 ft) 32% of shots will miss the hole irrespective of what the player - even Tiger Woods - does [28].

This is because the natural irregularities on a green that cannot be corrected for by the golfer impose the wobble on the ball's path which produces the observed spread.

Of course, there will be random errors due to the golfer hitting the ball slightly in error but these are human errors and are not included in this mathematical modelling.

The point to be understood here is that hitting a hole in one (Ace) or sinking a ball from a long putt is in part due to player skill and in part due to natural randomness outside the control of the player.

We need to understand the effect of randomness in golf before studying the results from this computer model.

This is perhaps best introduced in terms of the probability of hitting a 'hole-in-one' (Ace) shot.

Anyone hitting a hole-in-one from tee into a hole will inevitably believe that the shot was brilliant and the result of a lifetime's dedication, practice and skill.

Wrong! It's not! It's just a typical ball that just happens to go into the cup and no more special than any other ball.

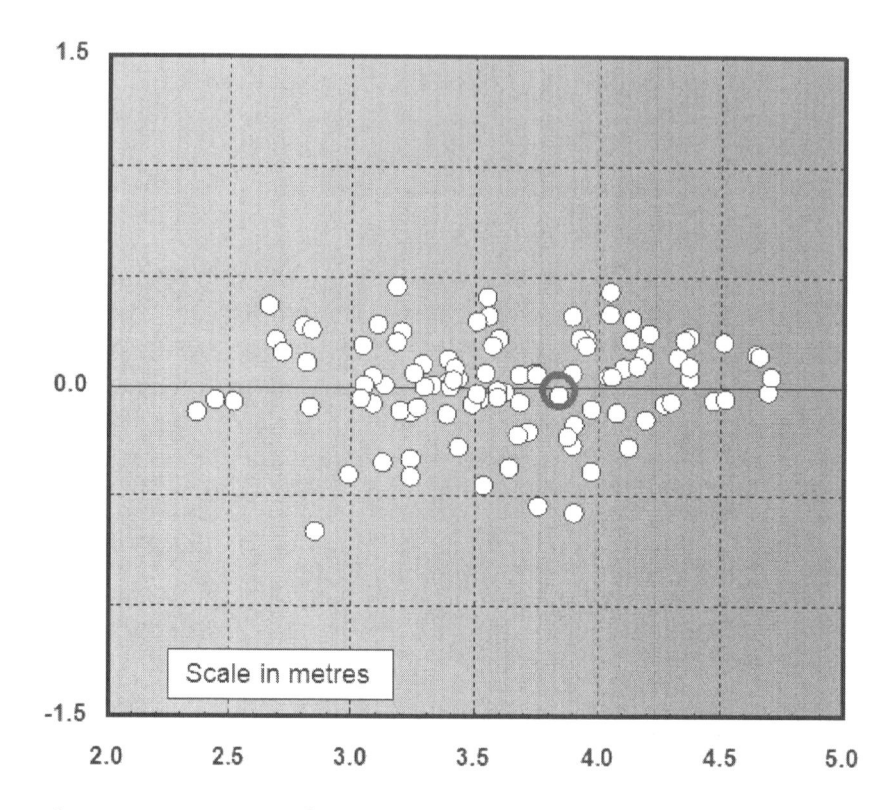

*Figure 47 - Scatter diagram for one hundred balls hit on a flat putting green.*

Figure 47 is Figure 45 reproduced but we now assume that there was a cup as shown by the circle [29].

Before the circle was superimposed on the diagram every white ball position was equally (in)significant. But now we have one ball position that lies in the circle but only because the circle has been arbitrarily placed where it is.

Suddenly, the ball that lies inside the circle becomes a 'hole in one' and the golfer would claim that she had made a brilliant putt when, in fact, it was just an ordinary shot that happened to go into the cup.

Sorry to deflate all readers who have made a long-range putt. In fact, on 5th October 2011 I sank a putt from 7 metres (23 ft) - by far the longest putt in my limited golfing experience. But, being a mathematician, I was not elated. I knew it was just a fluke.

Science does rather take the joy and boost to self esteem out of the game.

OK - so better players are more likely to hit a hole in one than bad players but, statistically, any player who can hit a ball from a tee to a green has the potential to hit a hole in one. It's just that the better player will need to hit fewer balls on average to achieve this feat.

The probability of hitting a hole in one has been studied and figures are available although difference sources give different estimates [30].

In 1999, *Golf Digest* reported,

*'One insurance company puts a PGA Tour professional's chances at 1 in 3,756 and an amateur's at 1 in 12,750'*

The *Golf Digest* study broke the odds down by quality of play:

- Tour player making an Ace: 3,000 to 1

- Low-handicapper making an Ace: 5,000 to 1

- Average player making an Ace: 12,000 to 1

Basically, hit a large enough number of golf balls and you may score a hole in one - or you may die before that rare random event occurs.

The mathematical model which will now be run to show its capabilities does not include randomness. This chapter has been included to warn the model user that the model results are for perfect greens and perfect golfing ability.

However, on some of the diagrams in the next chapter an indication is given of the likely effect of random errors on the results.

Finally, let's dispel some misconceptions of what makes a good putting shot.

# RANDOMNESS, SKILL AND MATHEMATICAL MODELLING

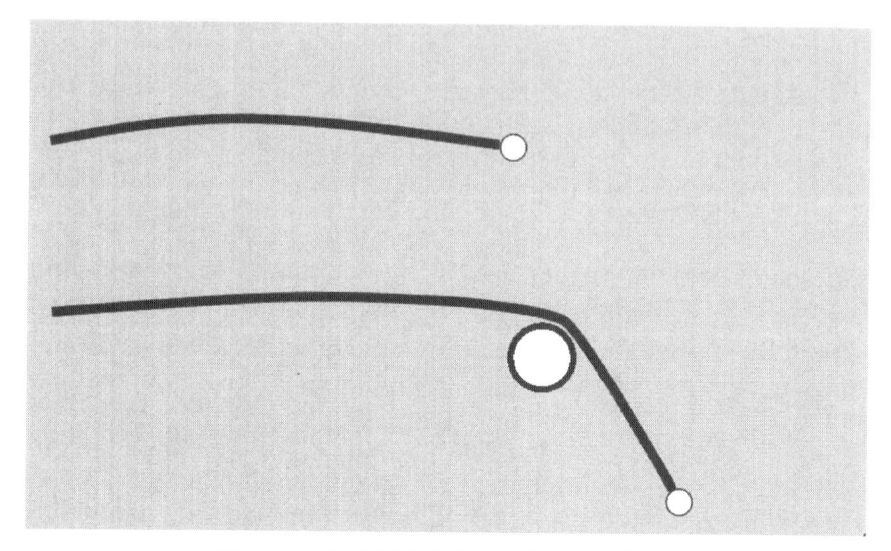

*Figure 48 - Which is the better shot?*

During a televised golf championship match a ball was hit from a bunker, over a ridge and onto the green where is rolled extremely close to the cup rim, rolled around it and finished about one metre from the cup as shown by the lower track in the above diagram.

The commentator was apoplectic with excitement!

*"What an outstanding shot!!!"* he yelled.

However, had the ball been hit wide and stopped one metre to the side of the cup - as in the upper track on the above figure - there would not have been the same excitement.

Why?

The ball would have ended up one metre from the cup in both cases so the final shot would have been equally easy.

Had that player hit a dozen balls out of that bunker they would have been scattered around the green. The fact that one of those shots went to the cup and skimmed around the rim was a combination of skill and good luck.

The relative importance of these two vital attributes in golf is a topic of endless debate and misunderstanding.

# 7. EXAMPLES OF WHAT THE MODEL CAN DO

## 7.1 Getting the ball into the cup

We saw in Chapter 5 that a ball heading towards the cup will not drop in unless its speed is high enough to reach the cup but also slow enough to drop into the cup without hitting the far side rim and bouncing out or rolling around the rim and setting off across the green on a path quite different from the approach path.

We saw that the ball will drop into the cup if the speed at the hole is less than

$$V_c = \left(2.03 - 1.24\,\varepsilon^2 + 0.63\,\varepsilon^4\right)\left(1 - \left|\frac{r}{54}\right|^{2.5}\right) \quad \text{(Equation 45)}$$

where the variables were defined earlier.

The mathematical model includes a check on whether a ball will be holed using the above equation as a criterion.

The diagram on the next page shows a typical model run where the ball goes in the cup.

## EXAMPLES OF WHAT THE MODEL CAN DO

```
          INITIAL SPEED (Vo) = 2.48  m/s
             INCLINATION (I) = 3.0   degrees
   INITIAL ANGLE (THETA(0)) = 0.0   degrees
             DRAG FACTOR (a) = 0.5   m/s^2
  COEFFICIENT OF RESTITUTION = 0.38
                SKID FACTOR = 0.52
                HOLE RANGE = 3.00  m
                HOLE ANGLE = -20.0 degrees
              TARGET RANGE = 3.80  m
     CLOSEST DISTANCE TO HOLE = 23   mm
                      HOLED? YES!
```

**ONLY THE NUMBERS IN BLUE SHADED CELLS SHOULD BE CHANGED**

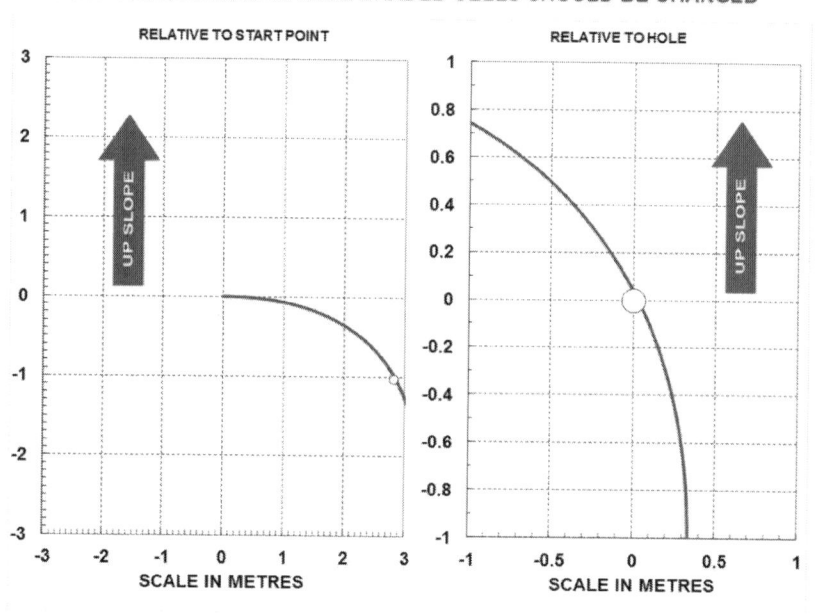

*Figure 49 - A typical model output*

Figure 49 shows a typical model output. At the top of the diagram are the fundamental parameters needed to define the problem and the chart shows the computed track of the ball.

In this example, the track passes over the cup at such a speed and angle that the ball drops into the cup in accordance with the equation derived earlier. The indicated value for closest distance of approach of the ball to cup changes colour if the centre of the ball passes over the rim of the cup.

The ball will only drop into the cup if the speed is in the correct range. If the ball does drop into the cup this is shown by a coloured marker as seen above.

# EXAMPLES OF WHAT THE MODEL CAN DO

Although the ball goes into the cup in this example, the model shows the track passing beyond the cup. This can be useful to show how far the ball would have travelled had it not dropped into the cup. This then indicates the difficulty of any subsequent shot to putt a ball which was not successfully holed.

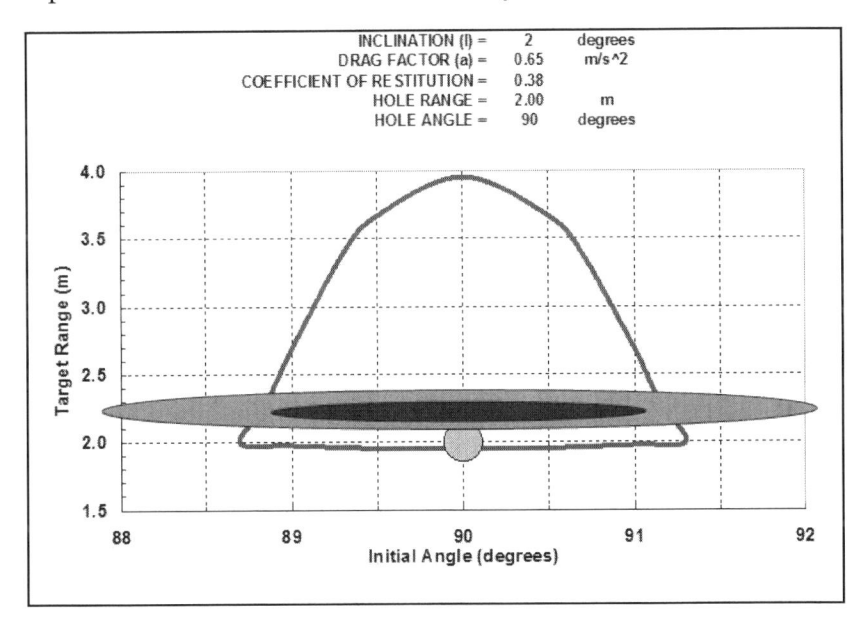

*Figure 50 - Tolerance for holing a shot directly up a 2 degree (3.5%) slope*

We have in Figure 50 a 2 degree (3.5% slope) green which has a value of '**a**' equal to 0.65 m/s² which is approximately a US Standard 'Fast' or a US Open 'Medium' rated green.

Figure 50 shows the result of varying the angle at which the ball sets off up the green and the target range of the ball. This latter is the range that the ball would travel if the cup were not in the ball's path. It is the point on the green that the player aims for the ball to stop if not holed.

The coefficient of restitution is typical of values measured by me on local golf course greens.

It can be seen that there is a 'Darth Vader' helmet shape outlined in within which the ball will drop into the cup.

The lower edge of the helmet is determined by the distance the ball will just travel and drop into the cup when it arrives at the cup centrally.

The upper boundary limit corresponds to the maximum speed that the ball would just drop into the cup. Any faster and it would bounce off the far rim and land back on the green.

The width of the 'helmet' is determined by the points at which the ball just stops on the extreme left or right edge of the rim - and then drops in.

The angular width of a cup at a range of 2 metres (6.6 ft) is about 3 degrees. However, the diagram shows an apparent angular width of about 2.6 degrees. This is because a ball hit at 1.3 degrees from the exact upslope path veers slightly away from the central track making the angular width of the cup seem smaller than expected. In general, the further the ball travels up the slope the smaller the angular width of the cup becomes beyond what is expected simply by geometry alone.

The 'helmet eye slits' are the loci for one and two standard deviations imposed by unpredictable variations in the green. We expect that 68% of putts by a world champion player would lie inside the inner ellipse and 95% within the outer ellipse.

We see that the best tactic is to try to place the ball about 0.25 metres (10 inches) beyond the cup. This should ensure the greatest chance of the ball reaching the cup and dropping in.

# EXAMPLES OF WHAT THE MODEL CAN DO

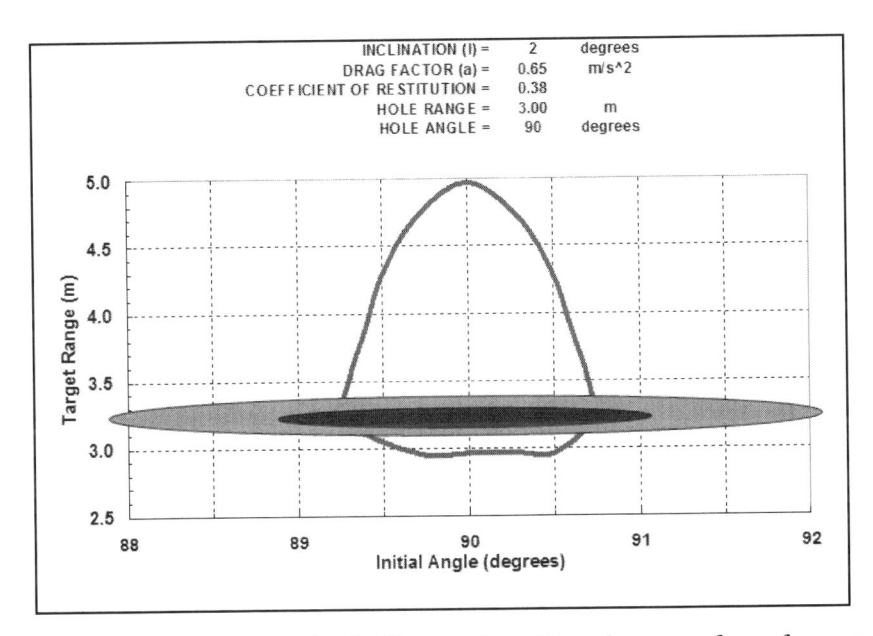

| | |
|---|---|
| INCLINATION (i) = | 2 degrees |
| DRAG FACTOR (a) = | 0.65 m/s^2 |
| COEFFICIENT OF RESTITUTION = | 0.38 |
| HOLE RANGE = | 3.00 m |
| HOLE ANGLE = | 90 degrees |

*Figure 51 - Tolerance for holing a shot directly up a slope from 3 metres range*

Figure 51 shows a similar calculation but this time for a 3 metre (9.8 ft) putt directly up a slope.

We see that the area is now much narrower and less than half of all shots will drop into the cup.

We now move on to investigate the tolerance and tactics for an across green putt.

We take a typical example of a 2 degree sloping green which has a value of '**a**' equal to 0.65 m/s$^2$ which is approximately a US Standard 'Fast' or a US Open 'Medium' rated green. The coefficient of restitution is typical of values measured by me on local golf course greens.

## EXAMPLES OF WHAT THE MODEL CAN DO

```
            INCLINATION =           2     degrees
            DRAG FACTOR =           0.65  m/s^2
COEFFICIENT OF RESTITUTION =        0.38   .
            SKID FACTOR =           0.52   .
            HOLE RANGE =            3.00   m
            HOLE ANGLE =            0     degrees
```

*Figure 52 - Tolerance chart for holing a ball rolling across the slope*

Figure 52 shows a tolerance chart for holing a golf ball for the geometry defined by the data on the figure.

The sausage shaped area enclosed by the boundary shows the combinations of target range (the distance aimed for by the golfer) and the angular offset which will result in a ball dropping into a cup.

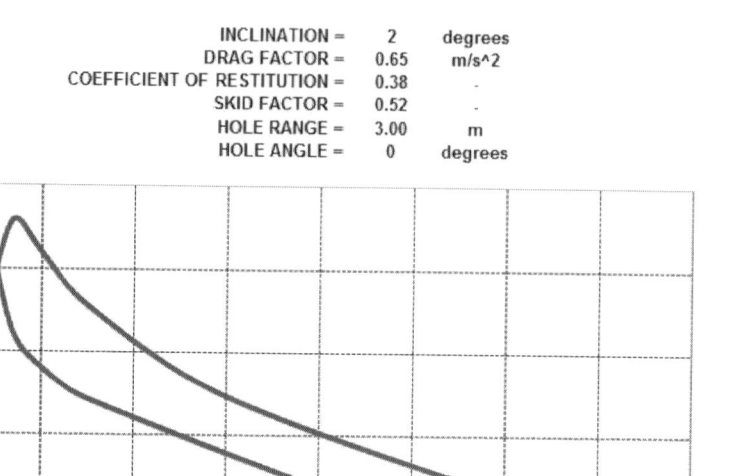

# EXAMPLES OF WHAT THE MODEL CAN DO

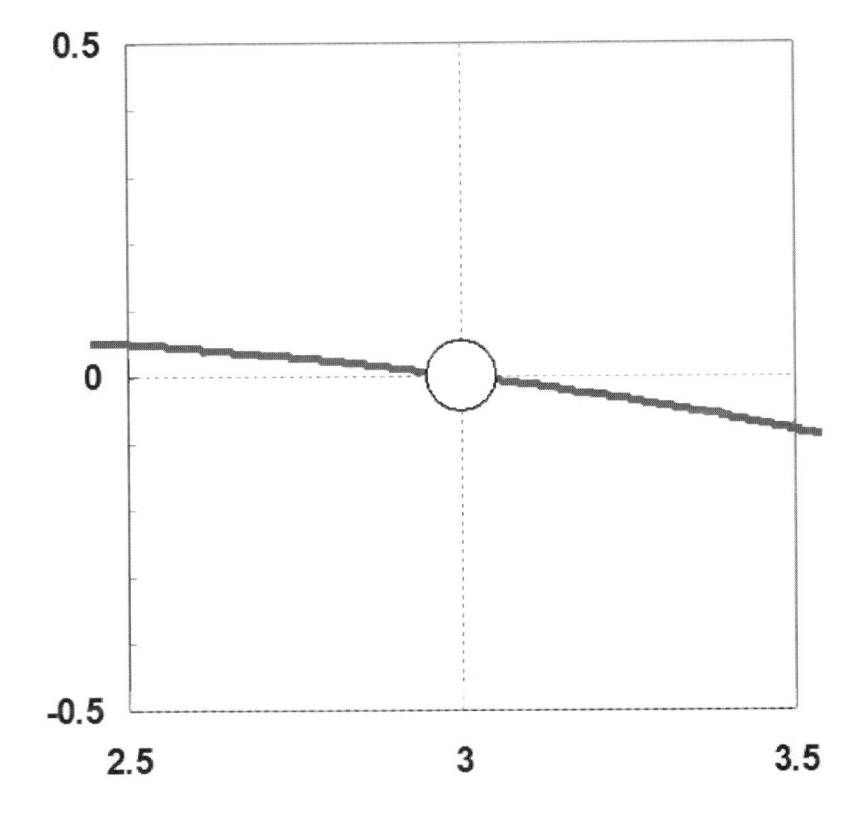

*Figure 53 - Conditions at extreme point 'A' on Figure 51*

Figure 53 shows the conditions at the extreme left-hand edge (A) of the sausage-shaped tolerance zone. This is the lowest offset angle that will still allow a ball to drop in the cup.

Because this is a high speed hit, if the ball were not to drop in the cup it would end up about 1.5 metres beyond the cup on account of its speed.

This is called a 'Charge' shot.

# EXAMPLES OF WHAT THE MODEL CAN DO

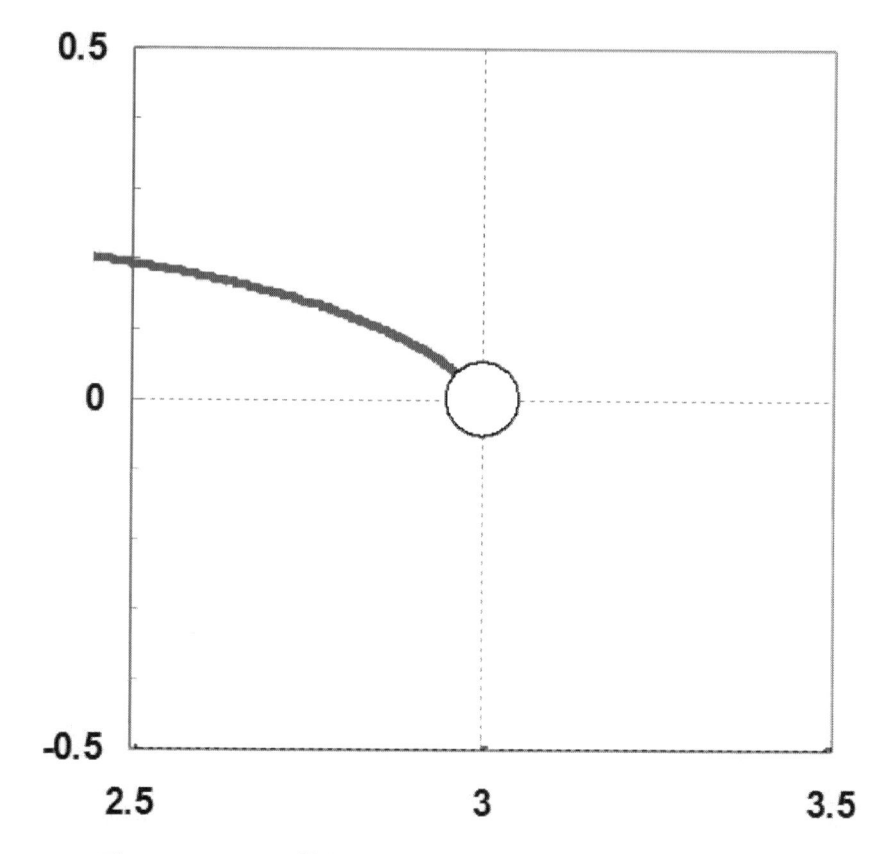

*Figure 54 - Conditions at extreme point 'B' on Figure 51*

The extreme right-hand extent of the sausage shaped area (B) corresponds to the slowest shot that will just reach the cup centrally and drop in. Figure 54 shows a close-up of the ball path close to the cup.

The area shown in Figure 52 enclosed by the curve is typical of tolerance zones although the shape and size will vary between green characteristics and the lie of the ball relative to the cup.

# EXAMPLES OF WHAT THE MODEL CAN DO

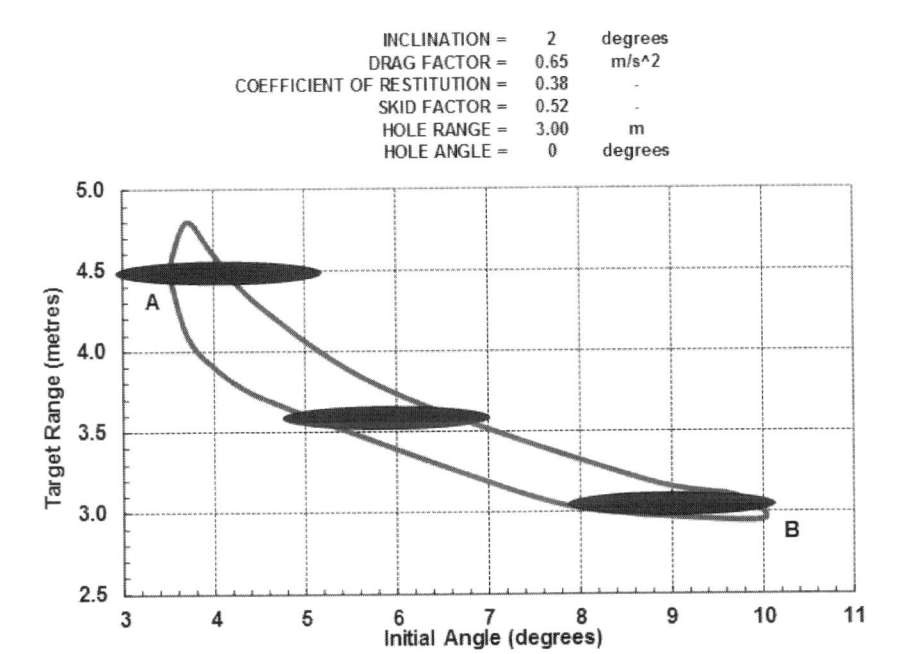

```
INCLINATION =              2     degrees
DRAG FACTOR =              0.65  m/s^2
COEFFICIENT OF RESTITUTION = 0.38  -
SKID FACTOR =              0.52  -
HOLE RANGE =               3.00  m
HOLE ANGLE =               0     degrees
```

*Figure 55 - Application of random errors to a three metre putt*

In reality, even an ideal player cannot 'read' a green perfectly and this is where the random variations measured by Frank Werner and Richard Grieg have to be factored in.

In Figure 55 I have taken the conditions shown on Figure 51 but superimposed the Standard Deviation natural to any green for balls hit towards three parts of the sausage area. In each ellipse the Standard Deviation in angle and range measured by Frank Werner and Richard Grieg has been applied; namely 1% in initial speed and 1.1 degrees in initial angle.

We see that it is better to go for the low speed, high offset (large break) shots on the right-hand of the sausage area because more of the ellipse falls within the locus.

This means aiming the ball to a point about 200 mm (8 in) beyond the cup.

This is very nearly the same tactic as for putts directly up or down slopes so it appears that a universal tactic for maximizing the probability of holing a putt is to aim at a point about 200 - 250 mm (8 - 10 in) beyond the cup taking into account the curvature of the path to the cup and the approach angle at the cup.

# EXAMPLES OF WHAT THE MODEL CAN DO

This tactic is additionally good because, if the ball is not holed it will end up close to the cup.

It should be clear by now that this validated mathematical model has many uses but the most important of these must be to investigate how to get the ball in the cup.

There are countless conditions that could be investigated and additional effects that could be included; the effect of wind is one that springs to mind.

As a finale for this Chapter I offer Figure 56 below which shows the path of a golf ball over a green which has a change of slope from up to down halfway between the putting point and the cup. Note how the model is able to predict the ball path curving first to the right as it rolls up the slope and then swerving to the left after it passes over the ridge and rolls down the slope towards the cup.

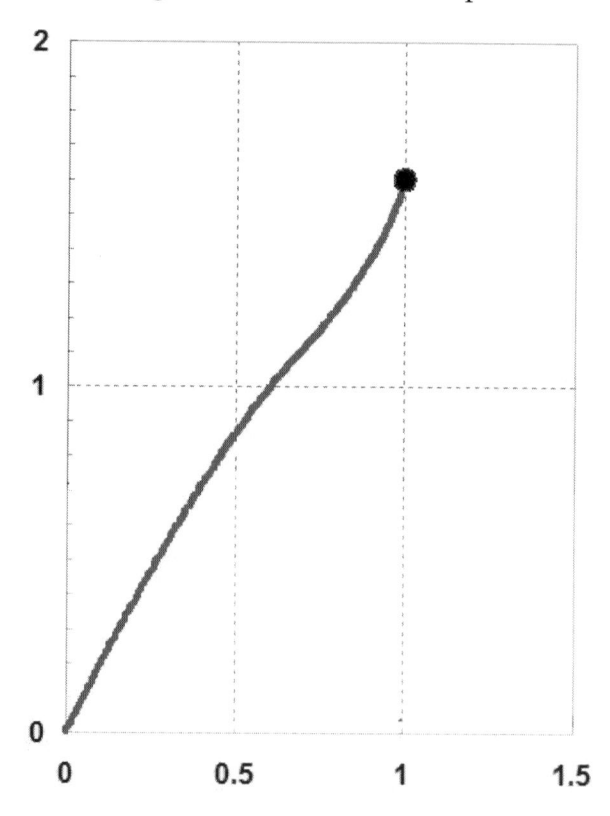

*Figure 56 - Prediction for a green having an up slope followed by a down slope profile*

# 8. WHAT IT ALL MEANS FOR THE NON-TECHNICAL PLAYER

## 8.1 Forget about those equations!

The book so far has shown that mathematics and physics can combine to describe the path of a ball over a putting green.

However, what the practical golfer needs to know is how to get the ball in the cup.

In this chapter the equations are interpreted in simply ways to help get that ball where you want.

Golf club rules vary and there may be some latitude in a few clubs over, for example, the use of handheld laser ranging devices to measure the distance to the pin. A laser device is also available for 'marking' the putting green to show the aim path of the ball. However no golf club that I know about would allow play on a green to stop while a player whips out a Stimpmeter (or homemade ramp as described in chapter 4) to measure the 'speed' and inclination of the green.

And yet, it is these two parameters that we need to know to get the ball into the cup.

So what players must do is to learn on practice putting greens to estimate their speed and inclination using a simple ramp and measure distances the ball travels using the golf shoes you are wearing.

Measure and remember the length of your shoe. This will be your ruler.

# WHAT IT ALL MEANS FOR THE NON-TECHNICAL PLAYER

Next make your ramp. Remember this is NOT a Stimpmeter which is a carefully designed and manufactured piece of precision engineering. What you have is a wooden ramp (such as dado rail) with a matchstick stuck 750 millimetres (30 in) from one end and enough sheets of cardboard glued adjacent to and 'uphill' of the matchstick to make the ball release when the inclination of the ramp is lifted to 20 degrees.

Remember, holing a golf ball is all about hitting the ball in the right direction and at the right speed as specified by the math equations in previous chapters of this book. If you can estimate well enough the inclination and 'speed' of the green then the ball may well go into the cup if it is hit at the requisite speed and direction.

What takes years of hard work is learning how to hit the ball correctly. Before the ball leaves the club face lie years of hard work and frustration. Once the ball leaves the putter face it is all math and physics.

## 8.2 Measuring and remembering inclination.

Nobody can claim that estimating the slope of a green is an easy talent to develop.

Douglas Brede carried out an experiment to test the ability of players to judge the slope of greens. He wrote [32]

*"Eyeballing the amount of slope - or lack of it - on a golf course is a tricky task, even for professional golfers. After all, golf course architects design greens with an optical illusion that makes slope difficult to judge. I took several students out to a green where I'd placed pairs of flags on various slopes. Most were unable to distinguish a 2.2% (1.2 degree) slope from level. Thus, don't rely on your sight to tell you if you're on a level area. You'll know you're on a level surface when the forward and reverse Stimpmeter readings differ by no more than six inches."*

On a practice putting green take your simple 20° homemade ramp as described in chapter 4 hidden in your golf bag.

When nobody is looking roll a ball using the ramp up the slope and down the slope and measure the distances travelled up ($J_U$) and down ($J_D$) using your known shoe length as your 'ruler'.

# WHAT IT ALL MEANS FOR THE NON-TECHNICAL PLAYER

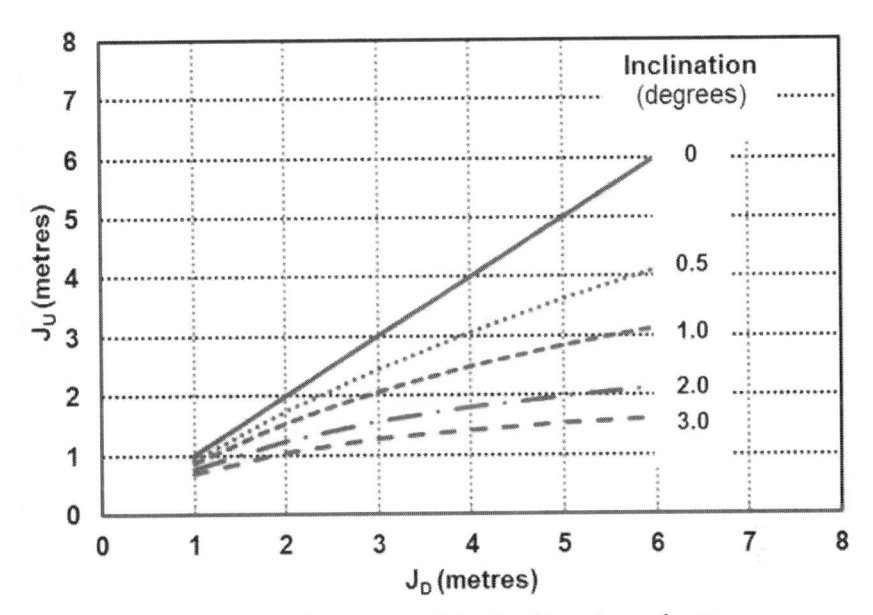

*Figure 57 - Estimation of the Inclination of a Green*

Figure 57 above allows you to read off the inclination of that green.

## *Example*

My shoe length is 0.30 metres (12 in) - see the chart in Appendix A.

Suppose that the rolling ball from my ramp travels 3.5 metres (11.5 ft) downhill and 2.5 metres (8.2 ft) uphill then from the above chart the inclination of the green is seen as 0.7 degrees (1.2%).

Make a note of the inclination of this green and move on to repeat this measurement for other practice greens.

Look at each of the practice greens and memorise the appearance of it so that it will become second nature to instantly know the inclination of a newly encountered green.

## 8.3 Measuring and remembering green speed.

On the same practice putting greens take your simple 20° homemade ramp and use the measurements up slope ($J_U$) and down slope ($J_D$) to estimate the speed of the greens using the chart below.

# WHAT IT ALL MEANS FOR THE NON-TECHNICAL PLAYER

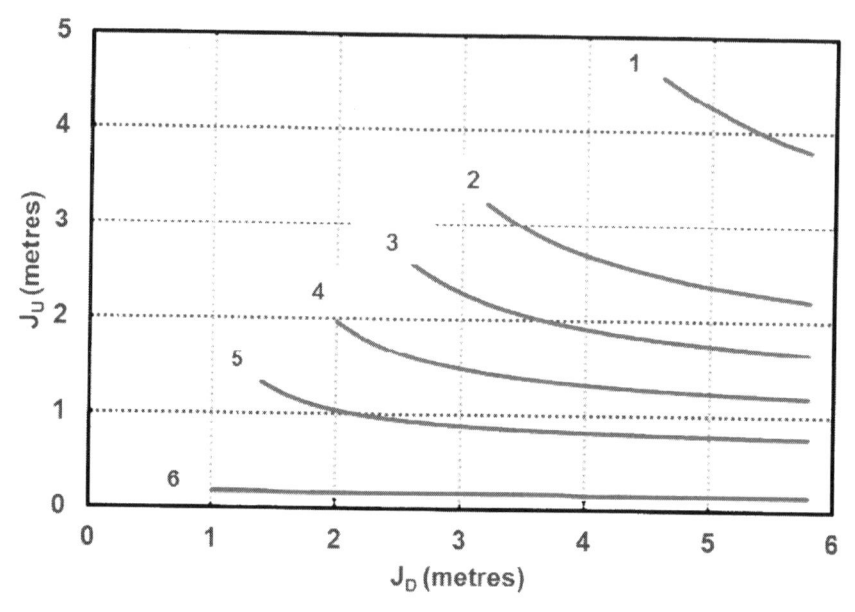

| Key To Chart | USGA Rating | US Open Rating | 'J' | 'a' m/s² |
|---|---|---|---|---|
| 1 | High Limit | | 15.0 (ft) / 4.45 (m) | 0.35 |
| 2 | | Fast | 10.5 (ft) / 3.19 (m) | 0.50 |
| 3 | | Medium | 8.5 (ft) / 1.58 (m) | 0.62 |
| 4 | Fast | Slow | 6.5 (ft) / (1.98 (m) | 0.81 |
| 5 | Medium | | 4.5 (ft) / 1.37 (m) | 1.18 |
| 6 | Slow | | 1.0 (ft) / 0.30 (m) | 5.29 |

*Figure 58 - Measurement of green speed*

Using the measurements made in the example above we see that 3.5 metres distance downhill and 2.5 metres up hill correspond to a speed about midway between Key curves 2 and 3, i.e., between 'FAST' and 'MEDIUM' on the US Open rating system with '**a**' about 0.56 m/s².

## 8.4 Two simple 'rules of thumb' to remember

On a simple inclined plane the golf balls will 'break' towards the down slope direction as shown in Figure 59.

# WHAT IT ALL MEANS FOR THE NON-TECHNICAL PLAYER

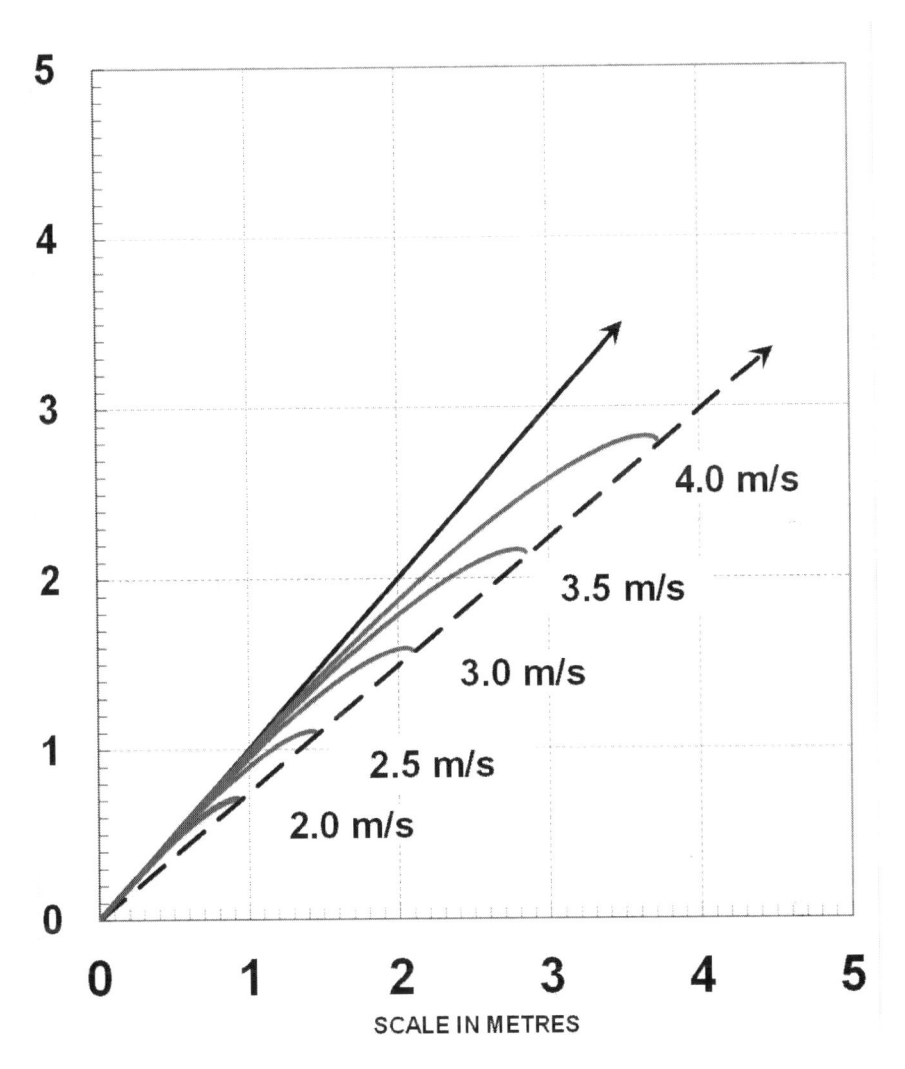

*Figure 59 - Paths of golf balls over a simple sloping green.*

The above figure shows the tracks of golf balls as predicted by the math and physics when hit in the same direction shown by the black unbroken arrow but at different speed.

First, note that the ball ends up on the same straight line drawn from the hit point. Although the balls are all aimed 45 degrees off the up-slope direction, they all finish up on a line 53 degrees from the up-slope direction irrespective of the speed with which they are hit.

This means that the offset angle is only dependent on the slope of

# WHAT IT ALL MEANS FOR THE NON-TECHNICAL PLAYER

the green, the angle of the cup off the upslope direction and the 'speed' of the green as measured by a Stimpmeter.

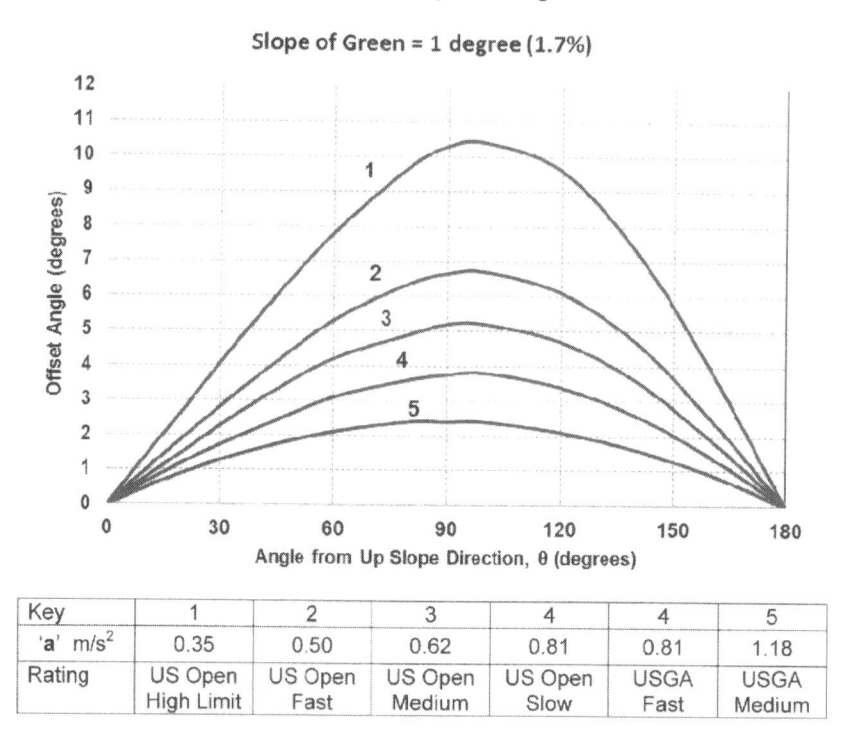

**Slope of Green = 1 degree (1.7%)**

| Key | 1 | 2 | 3 | 4 | 4 | 5 |
|---|---|---|---|---|---|---|
| 'a' m/s² | 0.35 | 0.50 | 0.62 | 0.81 | 0.81 | 1.18 |
| Rating | US Open High Limit | US Open Fast | US Open Medium | US Open Slow | USGA Fast | USGA Medium |

*Figure 60 - Variation of Offset Angle with Speed of Green.*

We see that the greatest offset is when the ball is hit more-or-less across the green.

This is obvious to all players.

It is worth remembering this variation however. For example, at 30 degrees from the up-slope direction (the one o'clock direction looking up the slope) the offset is approximately half that for the across slope direction.

# WHAT IT ALL MEANS FOR THE NON-TECHNICAL PLAYER

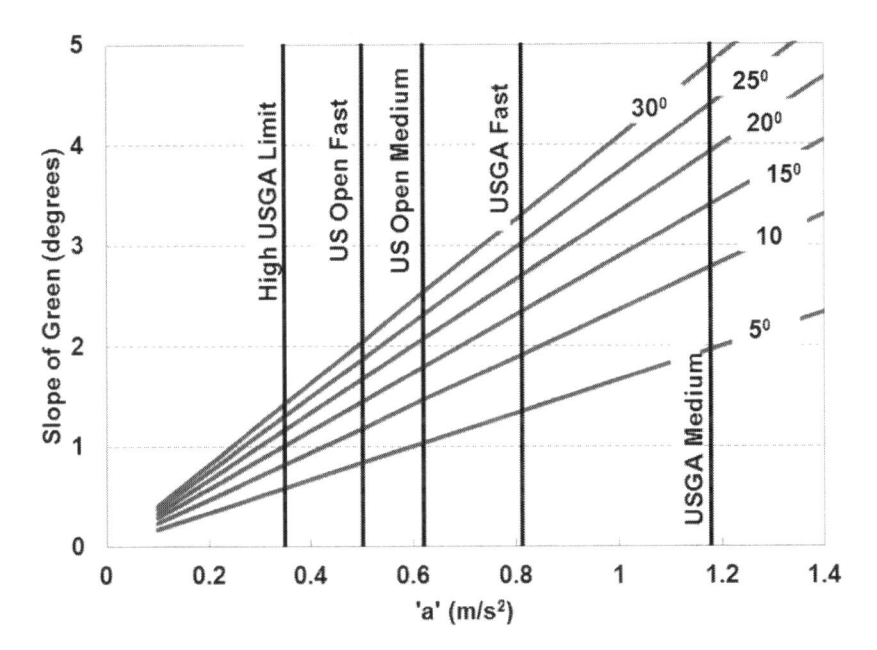

*Figure 61 - Variation of the across-green offset with speed of the green and slope*

Figure 61 shows how the maximum offset angle varies with the speed of the green 'a' and the slope inclination angle.

Using the experience gained on the practice putting green with the 20 degree ramp you should be able to judge the slope angle and green speed.

Let's say that the green inclination is judged to be 1.5 degrees and the speed about 'USGA Fast' corresponding to a value of '**a**' around 0.8 m/s².

From Figure 60 we find that the maximum offset across the green is about 7.5 degrees.

If the line to the hole is about 30 degrees from the up-slope direction then Figure 61 shows that the required offset is about 40% of the maximum offset; namely 40% of 7.5 degrees which is 3 degrees.

Hit the ball three degrees up the slope relative to the line to the cup and the ball will head off in the correct direction.

It may not drop in the cup but it will be pretty close!

Having sorted hitting the ball in the correct direction we now turn to the problem of hitting the ball such that it sets off with the correct speed.

The key here is to notice on Figure 58 that the distance travelled by the ball increases as the square of initial speed. In other words, hit a ball so that its starting speed is doubled it will go FOUR TIMES as far. This means that over hitting a ball is worse than under hitting it.

It is fortunate that the probability of a ball dropping into the cup is far less sensitive to ball speed than ball direction.

Look, for example, at Figure 50. The ball has to be hit such that the path passes over the rim of the cup. That is a very difficult problem requiring accuracy of hit direction within 1.2 degrees of the perfectly aimed shot.

However, the ball speed is very much less critical and the ball can be aimed to stop over a 2 metre (7 ft) range and still drop in the cup if the path is accurate. This corresponds to a tolerance on hit speed of 40%.

Thus, hitting the ball accurately along the correct track is paramount when hitting up or down a slope. Speed is much less critical.

That is why I have spent so much more time explaining how to use the charts and tables to aim the ball accurately and a lot less time on getting the ball speed optimised.

## 8.5 So it's not a simple inclined plane?

Although greens are usually close to being simple inclined planes for short to medium putts, for long putts the green can change slope over the run of the ball. Indeed, a well designed green will have challenging changes in slope between the ball and cup over distances of several metres.

The key to estimating how hard and in what direction to hit the ball depends on tracing the probable path by eye before hitting the ball. What simple "Rules of Thumb" can be offered?

First we need to appreciate how the speed of the ball changes with distance travelled.

# WHAT IT ALL MEANS FOR THE NON-TECHNICAL PLAYER

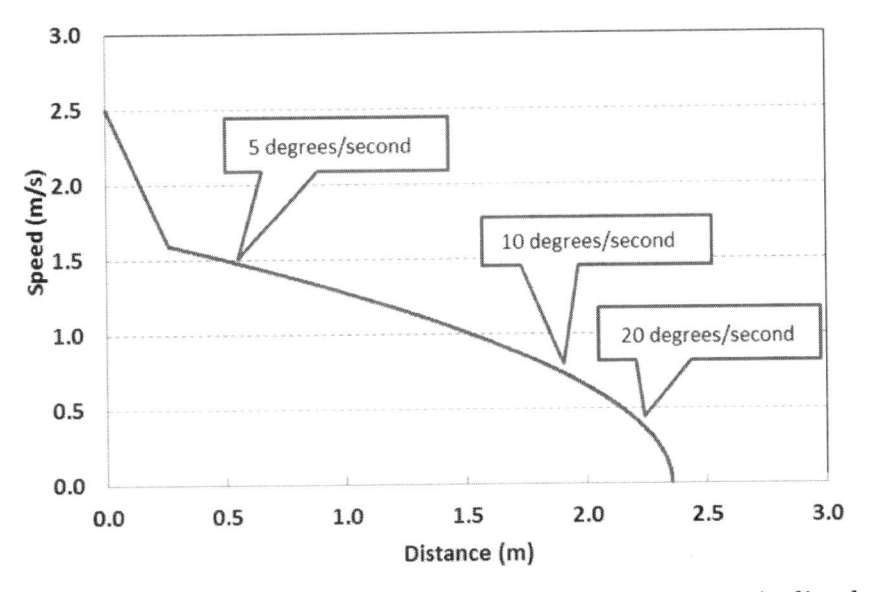

*Figure 62 A typical variation of ball speed across an inclined green*

The above figure shows a typical variation in ball speed across a simple inclined green with a slope of 1 degree (1.6%).

In fact, for a green where the slope changes slightly along the track of the ball the above general curve still applies.

The ball skids for about 250 mm (10 in) during which phase it slows down rapidly and loses about 40% of its initial speed. It then settles into a purely rolling mode of travel with the ball slowing down rapidly to a halt in the last half-metre.

It is well worth bearing the shape of the curve in Figure 62 in mind when sighting up a putt.

The ball will 'break' in the downslope direction as it travels. The rate that it curves left or right is inversely proportional to speed. Thus, when the ball speed has dropped to half its initial speed (i.e. by about 40% of the total distance) the ball will be curving twice as fast.

The rate at which the ball 'breaks' is shown on the above figure.

It is necessary to visualise that most of the 'break' occurs in the last one-third of the path to the cup and it this last part of the green that is most important.

# WHAT IT ALL MEANS FOR THE NON-TECHNICAL PLAYER

The first half of the track to the cup is of much lesser significance than the last quarter. It is in this final part of the path that the ball rapidly takes on its curving motion and this is where the putt goes wrong.

The frustration is in seeing a ball heading nicely on the up-slope line to the cup and watching it rapidly turning downslope to pass the cup.

# APPENDIX A

The table below allows you to convert between Imperial (feet and inches) and Metric (Metres) and vice versa.

# APPENDIX A

| FEET | \ | INCHES | | | | | | | | | | | |
|---|---|---|---|---|---|---|---|---|---|---|---|---|---|
| | 0 | 1 | 2 | 3 | 4 | 5 | 6 | 7 | 8 | 9 | 10 | 11 | 12 |
| 0 | 0.00 | 0.03 | 0.05 | 0.08 | 0.10 | 0.13 | 0.15 | 0.18 | 0.20 | 0.23 | 0.25 | 0.28 | 0.30 |
| 1 | 0.30 | 0.33 | 0.36 | 0.38 | 0.41 | 0.43 | 0.46 | 0.48 | 0.51 | 0.53 | 0.56 | 0.58 | 0.61 |
| 2 | 0.61 | 0.64 | 0.66 | 0.69 | 0.71 | 0.74 | 0.76 | 0.79 | 0.81 | 0.84 | 0.86 | 0.89 | 0.91 |
| 3 | 0.91 | 0.94 | 0.97 | 0.99 | 1.02 | 1.04 | 1.07 | 1.09 | 1.12 | 1.14 | 1.17 | 1.19 | 1.22 |
| 4 | 1.22 | 1.24 | 1.27 | 1.30 | 1.32 | 1.35 | 1.37 | 1.40 | 1.42 | 1.45 | 1.47 | 1.50 | 1.52 |
| 5 | 1.52 | 1.55 | 1.57 | 1.60 | 1.63 | 1.65 | 1.68 | 1.70 | 1.73 | 1.75 | 1.78 | 1.80 | 1.83 |
| 6 | 1.83 | 1.85 | 1.88 | 1.91 | 1.93 | 1.96 | 1.98 | 2.01 | 2.03 | 2.06 | 2.08 | 2.11 | 2.13 |
| 7 | 2.13 | 2.16 | 2.18 | 2.21 | 2.24 | 2.26 | 2.29 | 2.31 | 2.34 | 2.36 | 2.39 | 2.41 | 2.44 |
| 8 | 2.44 | 2.46 | 2.49 | 2.51 | 2.54 | 2.57 | 2.59 | 2.62 | 2.64 | 2.67 | 2.69 | 2.72 | 2.74 |
| 9 | 2.74 | 2.77 | 2.79 | 2.82 | 2.84 | 2.87 | 2.90 | 2.92 | 2.95 | 2.97 | 3.00 | 3.02 | 3.05 |
| 10 | 3.05 | 3.07 | 3.10 | 3.12 | 3.15 | 3.18 | 3.20 | 3.23 | 3.25 | 3.28 | 3.30 | 3.33 | 3.35 |
| 11 | 3.35 | 3.38 | 3.40 | 3.43 | 3.45 | 3.48 | 3.51 | 3.53 | 3.56 | 3.58 | 3.61 | 3.63 | 3.66 |
| 12 | 3.66 | 3.68 | 3.71 | 3.73 | 3.76 | 3.78 | 3.81 | 3.84 | 3.86 | 3.89 | 3.91 | 3.94 | 3.96 |
| 13 | 3.96 | 3.99 | 4.01 | 4.04 | 4.06 | 4.09 | 4.11 | 4.14 | 4.17 | 4.19 | 4.22 | 4.24 | 4.27 |
| 14 | 4.27 | 4.29 | 4.32 | 4.34 | 4.37 | 4.39 | 4.42 | 4.45 | 4.47 | 4.50 | 4.52 | 4.55 | 4.57 |
| 15 | 4.57 | 4.60 | 4.62 | 4.65 | 4.67 | 4.70 | 4.72 | 4.75 | 4.78 | 4.80 | 4.83 | 4.85 | 4.88 |
| 16 | 4.88 | 4.90 | 4.93 | 4.95 | 4.98 | 5.00 | 5.03 | 5.05 | 5.08 | 5.11 | 5.13 | 5.16 | 5.18 |
| 17 | 5.18 | 5.21 | 5.23 | 5.26 | 5.28 | 5.31 | 5.33 | 5.36 | 5.38 | 5.41 | 5.44 | 5.46 | 5.49 |
| 18 | 5.49 | 5.51 | 5.54 | 5.56 | 5.59 | 5.61 | 5.64 | 5.66 | 5.69 | 5.72 | 5.74 | 5.77 | 5.79 |
| 19 | 5.79 | 5.82 | 5.84 | 5.87 | 5.89 | 5.92 | 5.94 | 5.97 | 5.99 | 6.02 | 6.05 | 6.07 | 6.10 |
| 20 | 6.10 | 6.12 | 6.15 | 6.17 | 6.20 | 6.22 | 6.25 | 6.27 | 6.30 | 6.32 | 6.35 | 6.38 | 6.40 |

# APPENDIX B

## THE MATHEMATICS OF BOUNCING GOLF BALLS

### *B.1 Introduction.*

If a ball is rolling along a grass surface and meets an impediment (such as a worm cast, small hump, a windblown cigarette end, etc.,) the ball will briefly be kicked into the air and fly to land further up the course. What overall effect does this have on the distance travelled by the ball?

Perhaps the ball will travel further because it is relatively drag-free whilst in the air compared with rolling along the grass.

Maybe it will go less far because it is losing momentum by being deflected away from the grassy course.

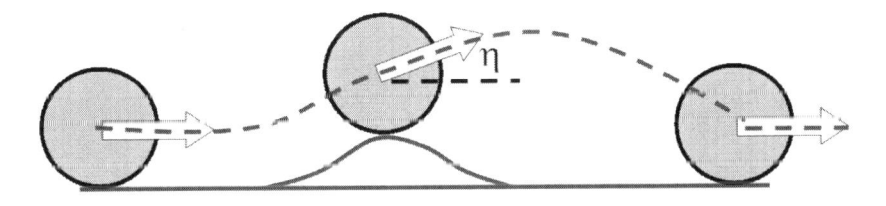

*Figure 63 - A stylised imperfection in the surface over which a balls rolls.*

Figure 63 shows a small hump in the surface of a golf course (fairway or green) which lifts the rolling ball and projects it upwards at a 'kick angle' $\eta$.

What we need to know is the loss or gain in distance travelled by

## B.2 The Model

To simplify the mathematics we imagine a golf ball rolling along the fairway or green having a drag 'a' (m/s²) being kicked up at an angle η, dropping back on the fairway or green and rolling to a stop.

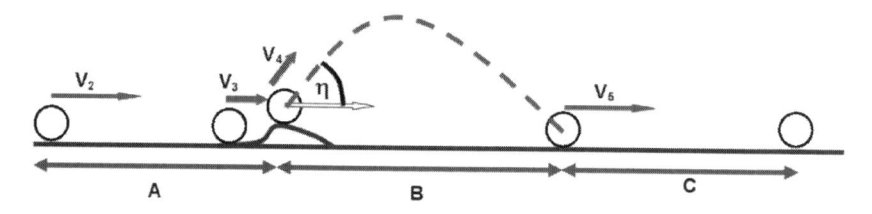

*Figure 64.-.A simplified hump showing the geometry.*

Let us assume that the ball starts rolling at speed $V_2$ at the left-hand edge of Figure 64. Having travelled to the foot of the hump the speed will have dropped to

$$V_3^2 = V_2^2 - 2aA \quad \text{(Equation 46)}$$

The ball will start up the slope with speed

$$V_4 = V_3 \cos(\eta) \quad \text{(Equation 47)}$$

The ball then flies through the air and lands distance **B** from the hump. The aerodynamic drag on the ball whilst in the air is neglected.

The time of flight (assuming the height of the hump is small compared with the height of the bounce) is given by

$$t_1 = \frac{2V_4 \sin(\eta)}{g} \quad \text{(Equation 48)}$$

From this we find the distance **B** to be

$$B = \frac{2V_4^2 \cos(\eta)\sin(\eta)}{g} \quad \text{(Equation 49)}$$

Also

$$V_5 = V_4 \cos(\eta) \quad \text{(Equation 50)}$$

# THE MATHEMATICS OF BOUNCING GOLF BALLS

The ball then rolls to a stop over distance **C** such that

$$C = \frac{V_5^2}{2a} \quad \text{(Equation 51)}$$

The total distance travelled (**A** + **B** + **C**) is a measure of the effect of the 'kick' in the ball's path when compared with the straight distance without any upward 'kick'.

## B.3 Model Validation

The above equations were checked by rolling a golf ball down a ramp on my living room carpet and directing it towards, and over, the small ramp shown below.

*Figure 65 - The artificial obstruction that gives the ball a 'kick'*

The angle at which the ball is launched into the air by this ramp is 32 degrees.

The two figures below show the measurement, for two different values of '**A**' compared with the values predicted by the above equations.

It can be seen that the model predictions work well.

# THE MATHEMATICS OF BOUNCING GOLF BALLS

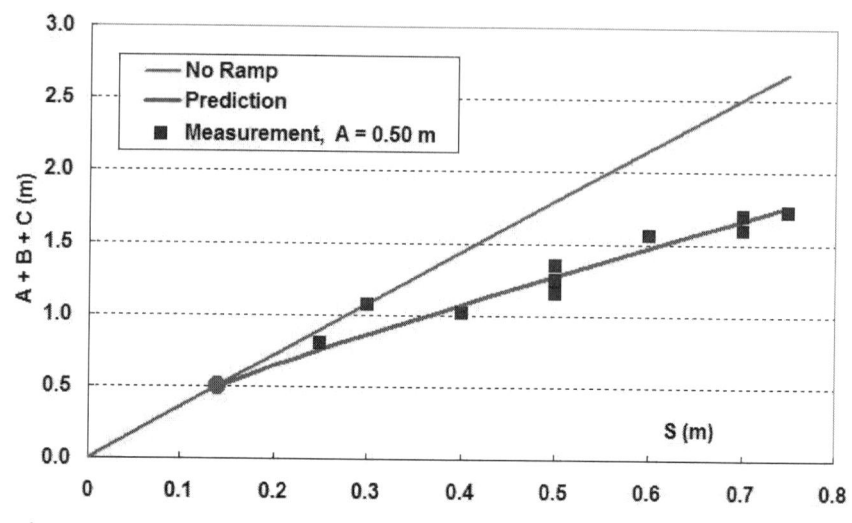

*Figure 66 - Comparison of measurements with predictions from the model.*

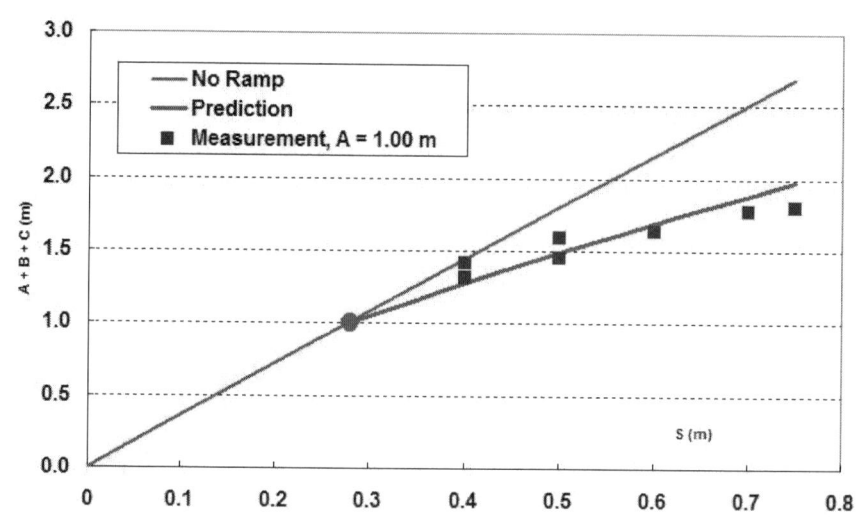

*Figure 67 - Comparison of measurements with model predictions.*

In both of the above figures the upper curve is the distance the balls would have travelled without the ramp using the equations developed in Chapter 2 and the measured value of drag '**a**'.

It can be seen that the overall distance travelled by the golf ball is reduced by the ramp.

Where the predicted (lower) curve and the 'No Ramp' curve meet (the circle) corresponds to the distance the ball would travel just to

# THE MATHEMATICS OF BOUNCING GOLF BALLS

reach the foot of the ramp but not be affected by it.

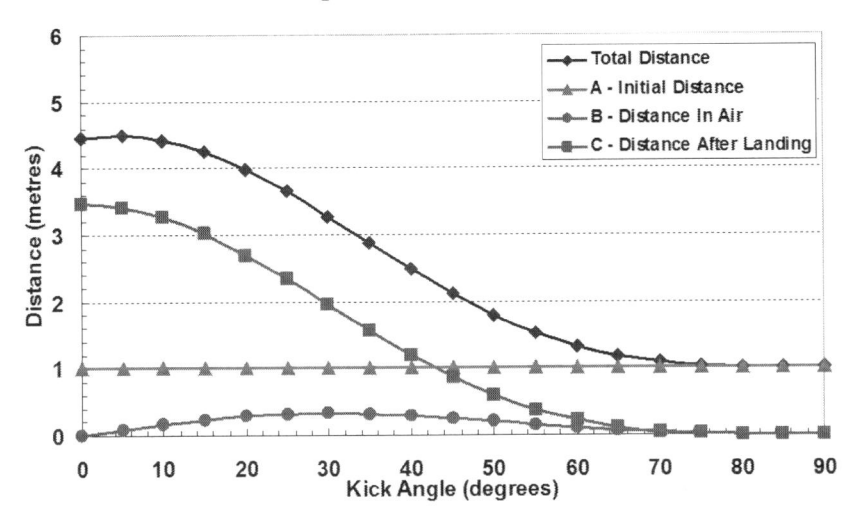

*Figure 68 - Predictions for $a = 0.7\ m/s^2$, $V_2 = 2.5\ m/s$, $A = 1.0\ m$*

Figure 68 shows the predicted total distance run by a ball for the conditions stated in the figure caption.

It can be seen that there is an increase in total distance travelled for a Kick Angle ($\eta$) lower than about 10 degrees but the effect is small.

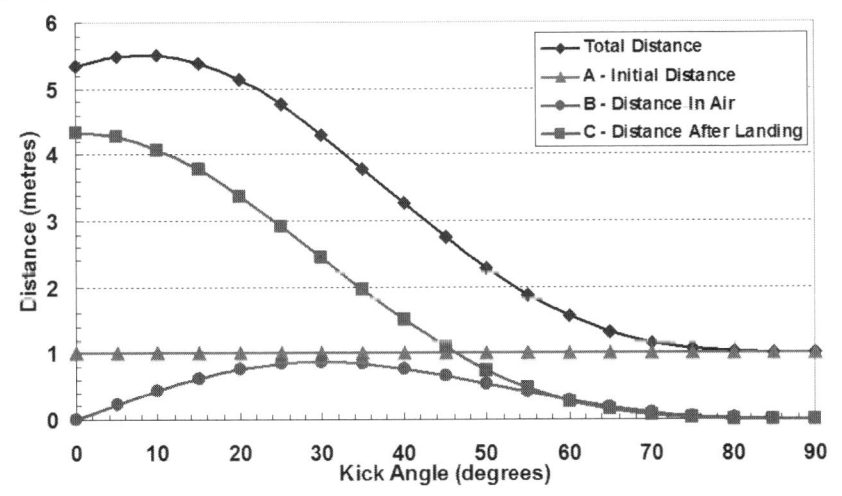

*Figure 69 - Predictions for $a = 1.5\ m/s^2$, $V_2 = 4.0\ m/s$, $A = 1.0\ m$*

Figure 69 shows a more extreme case of a high drag surface and a faster initial ball speed. The previous conclusion still applies;

# THE MATHEMATICS OF BOUNCING GOLF BALLS

namely that there is a very slight increase in range run by the ball for kick angles up to about 15 degrees but the advantage is not large.

In reality, when the ball kicks into the air and lands it will bounce and make one or more further flights.

The path in the air on any second or subsequent bounce is determined by the Coefficient Of Restitution (COR) of the grass surface ε. This is the ratio of the vertical component of the ball speed before and after hitting the grass surface.

The description of the Coefficient Of Restitution and its measurement are described earlier.

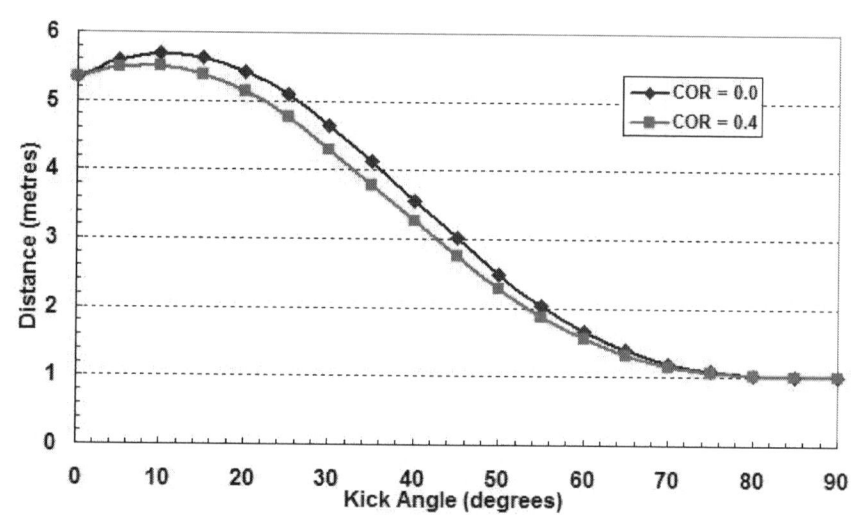

*Figure 70 - The effect of multiple bouncing after 'kicking' off an impediment*

Figure 70 shows the effect of including multiple bounces on the fairway or putting green as a function of whether the ball bounces or not.

It can be seen a 'bouncy' grass surface causes a reduction in distance travelled but this is hardly significant.

The conclusion from this Chapter of the overall study is that a 'kick' that sends a rolling ball into the air will generally not increase the overall distance travelled although there is a scarcely significant increase in distance where the ball bounces at an angle less than about 10 - 15 degrees from the horizontal.

# REFERENCES

1. See Malcolm Gladwell's book *'Outliers'* http://en.wikipedia.org/wiki/Outliers_(book)

2. Mathematicians use a unit of radians for measuring angles. One radian is about 57 degrees. Golfers sometimes refer to the slope of a green in percentage gradient. A slope of 1% corresponds to an angle of about 0.57 degrees.

3. *"The trajectory of a ball in lawn bowls"* Rod Cross. Physics Department, University of Sydney, Sydney 2006, Australia Available as http://www.physics.usyd.edu.au/~cross/PUBLICATIONS/2.%20LawnBowls2.PDF

4. *"The trajectory of a ball in lawn bowls"* Rod Cross. Physics Department, University of Sydney, Sydney 2006, Australia Available as http://www.physics.usyd.edu.au/~cross/PUBLICATIONS/2.%20LawnBowls2.PDF

5. http://en.wikipedia.org/wiki/List_of_moments_of_inertia

6. Some investigators define a Friction Factor which is equivalent to **a/g**.

7. I am in illustrious company! Galileo rolled balls down ramps to derive his famous Laws of Motion which were expanded by Isaac Newton into the formulation of dynamics which is used universally today to describe the world in which we live. Galileo's balls rolling down ramps created the dividing line between medieval ignorance and the Age of Enlightenment.

8. Purists would call this an acceleration of -**a** m/s$^2$

9. Included in the drag is air resistance as the ball rolls along the surface. This is naturally included in the measurements. However, it can be shown by calculation that air drag is negligible at putting speeds. Furthermore, because air drag varies as the square of speed and the measured drag varies as independent of speed it follows that the experiments described here confirm air drag to be unimportant.

10. Included in the drag is air resistance as the ball rolls along the surface. This is naturally included in the measurements. However,

# REFERENCES

it can be shown by calculation that air drag is negligible at putting speeds. Furthermore, because air drag varies as the square of speed and the measured drag varies as independent of speed it follows that the experiments described here confirm air drag to be unimportant.

11. http://en.wikipedia.org/wiki/Coriolis_effect#Applied_to_Earth

12. http://www.youtube.com/watch?v=eayNQKBJD0A

13. Reproduced on page 49 in H. A. Templeton, *"Vector Putting the Art and Science of Reading Greens"* (1984) Vector Putting Inc.

14. *"The Proof Is In The Putting"* Scott K. Perry *"The Physics Teacher"* Vol. 40, October 2002, 411 - 414

15. http://en.wikipedia.org/wiki/Stimpmeter

16. http://www.csgnetwork.com/stimpmetercalc.html

17. Brede, A. Douglas *USGA Green Section Record*, November/December 1990 - see http://www.usga.org/course_care/articles/management/greens/Measuring-Green-Speed-on-Sloped-Putting-Greens/

18. *"Newton on the Tee"* published by Simon and Schuster, paperback edition 2008 page 105

19. B. W. Holmes, *"Putting: How a Golf Ball and Hole Interact,"* Am. J. Phys. **59**, 129 (1991)

20. Although the Coefficient of Restitution (COR) is a general term used in science and engineering, it is now widely used in golf science where it defines the extra speed given to a ball by a flexible surface to a golf club - see http://en.wikipedia.org/wiki/Coefficient_of_restitution

21. From http://en.wikipedia.org/wiki/Coefficient_of_restitution

22. B. W. Holmes, *"Putting: How a Golf Ball and Hole Interact,"* Am. J. Phys. **59**, 129 (1991)

23. I prefer to call the curve 'Gaussian' to recognize the genius of Carl Friedrich Gauss - widely acknowledged as the greatest mathematician of all time after Isaac Newton.

24. http://en.wikipedia.org/wiki/Normal_distribution

25. http://en.wikipedia.org/wiki/Central_limit_theorem

# REFERENCES

26. http://en.wikipedia.org/wiki/Standard_deviation

27. Quoted in John Zumerchik's book *""Newton on the Tee"* published by Simon and Schuster, paperback edition 2008 page 209.

28. This assumes that the angular distribution of random errors due to the green is Gaussian in which case 32% of shots will lie outside the Standard Deviation.

29. The sizes of the balls and cup are not to the correct scale.

30. http://golf.about.com/od/faqs/f/holeinoneodds.htm

31. Quoted in John Zumerchik's book *""Newton on the Tee"* published by Simon and Schuster, paperback edition 2008 page 209.

32. Brede, A. Douglas USGA Green Section Record, November/December 1990 - see http://www.usga.org/course_care/articles/management/greens/Measuring-Green-Speed-on-Sloped-Putting-Greens/

# REFERENCES

Made in the USA
Middletown, DE
25 February 2016